Getting Your
Baby to Sleep the

Baby
Sleep
Trainer
Way

NATALIE WILLES

ISBN: 978-0-9990867-0-4

Illustrator: Graphic design by Eliza Frye

For Olive and Milo: Without you there would be none of this.

CONTENTS

INTRODUCTION

If you're reading this book, you likely fall into one of two categories: You're either a type-A, get-'er-done parent who is trying to preempt any sleep problems by tackling them early or preventing them before they start, or you are the parent of an infant or toddler, and completely and utterly exhausted because your child is struggling to sleep well. Either way, this book is for you!

I'd like to first address the latter group. I've spent the better part of the last five years working with hundreds of families across the world to solve their children's sleep issues. Parents come to me having read multiple books, spoken to dozens of friends, and scoured the entire Internet trying to figure just *how* to help their beautiful and precious child sleep through the night and take healthful, restorative naps during the day. So many families find success to be completely elusive, and determining the right solution is complicated by the fact that nearly every piece of information a parent reads or hears is in direct conflict with the next. Add a tremendous lack of sleep for parents and baby, and it's not hard to see why sleep issues seem to compound so quickly.

Here's my secret: I was once like you! I dog-eared, highlighted, and tagged multiple sleep books before my first child, Olive, was born eight years ago, and I remember how it felt for days to turn into weeks as I desperately tried to find the formula that would result in something that I had thought would be easy and natural—sleep!

To those of you in the first category, who are reading this in preparation for your new baby, I commend you. Understanding the principles in this book will help you avoid many of the long-term issues that families tend to endure when it comes to sleep. You won't be able to avoid needing to sleep train your baby, for reasons I will go into in the coming chapters, but it will be accomplished more easily by not only knowing what to expect, but also when and how to appropriately deal with issues when they do inevitably arise.

For anyone who has already read a stack of books, believe me, I know there's a lot of information out there, and I also know that sleep experts tend to come across as extremely authoritative, making you feel like their way is the *only* way. I am not here to tell you that the Baby Sleep Trainer Method is the only way, and I'm not even going to tell you that it's the *best* way (although hundreds of clients have told me that it's been true for them). I am here to tell you that, when applied consistently, the Baby Sleep Trainer Method works for almost every child, and it usually resolves sleep problems with the *least amount of overall crying* out of any popular approach. I'll make an evidence-backed case for everything I ask you to do, and guide you through any blip and bump you may experience along the journey. All you need to be successful is patience and consistency.

HOW TO USE THIS BOOK

THERE IS ONE principle that is key to understanding the Baby Sleep Trainer Method, and that is that nearly all sleep issues arise out of a child's inability or unwillingness to fall asleep unassisted. Nearly every family that calls me with a four-month-old, a three-year-old, or any age in between, shares a single trait: a child who is dependent on something or someone else to fall asleep. (There is the rare child who struggles with sleep due to something as simple as napping too much each day, causing them to wake excessively at night, or waking too early in the morning because they don't have blackout curtains in their bedroom windows. But these are few and far between.)

Generally, parents come to me with a variation on these issues. Their child:

1. takes a long time to fall asleep (via rocking, nursing, or needing someone to lie next to them);

2. wakes immediately or shortly after having been put down in their crib;

3. wakes repeatedly at night, needing some form of assistance to fall back to sleep, like a pacifier, feeding, rocking, etc.; or

4. won't fall asleep easily for naps, skips naps altogether, naps for only short periods of time, has no consistent nap schedule, or only naps while moving in a stroller, carrier, or car seat.

At first glance, these appear to be unrelated problems, but upon closer inspection, it becomes clear that the trait they *actually* share is that they all have to do with a child not knowing how to fall asleep on their own.

A child who takes a long time to settle into sleep for naps or at night is usually just struggling with the method being used to "get them" to fall asleep in the first place. That is, the child naturally wants to lie down, close their eyes, and fall asleep, but they only *know* how to fall asleep with assistance, be it rocking, nursing, strolling, or sleeping next to someone else. If a child has had help, they often wake up once that help is taken away (for example, many babies wake up the moment a parent places them in their crib, even though they appeared deeply asleep while being held).

Parents often mistake frequent night wakings as an indication that their child is not yet "sleeping through the night," or, conversely, if they do not hear their baby crying overnight, that they are. In fact, all humans wake regularly throughout the night (generally, after completing each sleep cycle, which occurs every thirty to sixty minutes for infants). Children who have assistance at bedtime will often need it again each time they wake. There are even children who fall asleep easily at bedtime but seek assistance during night wakings and for naps. At night—especially at bedtime—the body's hormonal cycles make it somewhat easier to fall asleep, but children who are reliant on external help struggle to sleep at bedtime can have a very, very hard time falling back to sleep after they complete a cycle.

I go into this much detail because I want to show parents that the primary goal of sleep training is to teach a child to go from being 100 percent awake to 100 percent asleep without any assistance. It's really that simple. Now that we have identified the root of nearly all sleep issues, the solution becomes both more obvious and easier to attain.

Since our primary goal is to ensure that children are falling asleep unassisted for naps and at bedtime, this book provides clear instructions on implementing a program that will achieve exactly that. First, I'll make a concise, but detailed and science-based, case for the importance of training exactly as laid out in this book. I'll also address the most common impediment for parents (spoiler alert: it's crying!), and, for those with newborns, I'll give extensive direction on what can be done in the early weeks of life to help baby and parents get as much sleep as possible. You'll also learn the only four things that are truly necessary to have in your child's bedroom in order to promote successful sleep training. Since consistency is key, I'll give you a few important tips to make sure you are able to remain steady from start to finish.

In the Baby Sleep Trainer Method, sleep training *always* starts at bedtime. Other than some small preparations in the child's sleeping area, no accommodations are generally necessary before jumping in (other than checking in with your pediatrician to make sure your baby is ready to start learning how to fall asleep on their own). Studies have shown that falling asleep unassisted at the start of the night leads to fewer wakings throughout the rest of the night, and, in my extensive experience, I have found a profound benefit to starting sleep training at bedtime, more than at any other time of day or night.

After your child falls asleep successfully at bedtime, you can move through my instructions on how to work through night wakings, including how to keep or eliminate night feedings. Then you will learn how to ensure that your child starts each day at around the same time—this is *key* to a consistent and healthy nap schedule. Finally, we'll discuss how to teach your child to nap on their own, and an age-appropriate napping schedule. You'll also learn how to troubleshoot common issues and deal with setbacks like illness, teething, and travel, plus how to implement the Baby Sleep Trainer method for twins and multiples.

Are you ready? Because I am! And I'll be with you every step of the way.

ARE YOU STRUGGLING

for the time to read or
the energy to concentrate?

Trust me, I understand!

Would you rather watch a video
series covering the entire Baby Sleep
Trainer method in detail — all in
under an hour of your time? Plus
have the option of follow up support?

Check out my online
training series on
www.babysleeptrainer.com

THE SCIENCE OF SLEEP

WHEN I STARTED my business in 2011, I knew that I had a knack for sleep training—having both learned what worked with my own child and helped many of my friends get their babies to sleep—and I'd read every book I could find on the subject. I studied sociology in college, so I also knew the value of reading and correctly interpreting scientific data, and I wanted to make sure to always stay up-to-date on the latest studies. Over the last several years, vast amounts of data have come out supporting the importance of sleep for a healthy body. To that end, I'd like to discuss some of the science about children and their sleeping patterns.

One thing that's important to keep in mind is that sleep patterns in babies are much different than in older children and adults. First, let's break down what's happening during sleep. While a human sleeps, their brain and body go through five distinct stages, characterized by either REM (rapid eye movement) sleep or NREM (non-rapid eye movement) sleep.[1] Stages 1 and 2 are light sleep, 3 and 4 are deep sleep, and 5 consists exclusively of REM sleep. REM sleep is when dreams occur, energy is restored to the brain and body, and the brain is generally active—so active that an EEG would show similar amounts of activity to an awake brain! NREM sleep is even more restorative; it's when the body repairs itself and releases a host of incredible hormones, including those that regulate growth, muscle development, and appetite—all imperative for growing babies.

In the first six months of a baby's life, their sleep stages are not fully developed, so researchers distinguish between "active" and "quiet" sleep instead.[2] Active sleep is a lot like REM sleep and quiet sleep is, you guessed it, a lot like NREM sleep. During active sleep, babies (like adults) can be woken very, very easily, while quiet sleep is when they seem like they can sleep through just about anything. While adults spend only about 25 percent of each night in REM sleep,[3] infants under the age of six months spend

---

1 Mary A. Carskadon and William C. Dement, "Monitoring and Staging Human Sleep," in *Principles and Practice of Sleep Medicine*, 5th ed., ed. Meir H. Kryger, Thomas Roth, and William C. Dement (St. Louis: Elsevier Saunders, 2011), 16-26. doi:10.1002/ppul.1950080117.

2 Thomas F. Anders and Pearl Weinstein, "Sleep and Its Disorders in Infants and Children: A Review." *Pediatrics* 50(2) (1972): 312-24.

3 "What Happens When You Sleep?" National Sleep Foundation, accessed March 11, 2017, https://sleepfoundation.org/how-sleep-works/what-happens-when-you-sleep.

equal portions of their sleep cycles, which last between thirty and fifty minutes, in REM and NREM sleep.[4] By month six, REM sleep decreases to about 30 percent of each cycle.

Stages of Sleep

very lightly asleep

This is when parents typically think their child is asleep, but it is only a very light sleep. Baby will usually wake up as soon as they are put down in their crib. This stage can last from 10-20 minutes.

deepest stages of sleep

This is the most restorative stage of sleep when the body repairs itself and releases essential hormones, including those that regulate growth, muscle development, and appetite.

lightest stage of sleep (REM)

This is the stage when dreams occur and energy is restored to the brain and body. It is also the lightest stage of sleep making it very easy for baby to be woken up.

This next point is extremely important and will come up again and again throughout this book. After an interval of quiet sleep in babies six months and younger, or after completion of a full NREM/REM five-stage cycle in older babies and toddlers, children will either enter another sleep cycle—or they will wake up. No matter how many books on sleep I read and how many how-to-sleep-train blog posts I encounter, I rarely see this point made: *An overwhelming*

---

4 Eric H. Chudler, "What is Sleep... And Why Do We Do It?" *Neuroscience for Kids*, accessed March 11, 2017, http://faculty. washington.edu/chudler/sleep.html.

majority of sleep-related issues, for very young infants to school-aged children, is related to a child's inability or unwillingness to fall asleep unassisted. Most babies with sleep issues are reliant on *something* to fall asleep, whether that's a pacifier, rocking chair, car seat, stroller, or twirling Mom's hair, and when they finish a cycle with light-sleep REM, they are unable to fall back into deep sleep without that same assistance.

As the night goes on, infants and adults alike spend more and more time in REM sleep and less and less time in NREM sleep. This means that as morning approaches, your child's REM sleep (stage 5) will occupy more and more time out of a given cycle. While the *average* amount of each cycle might be 50/50 active/quiet for very young babies and 30/70 REM/NREM sleep in older babies, children, and adults, more minutes are spent in deep sleep stages early in the night, and more minutes are spent in very active/light sleep stages as night turns into morning. This is why so many families find that the first part of their child's sleep is relatively uneventful, with few or no wakings, but over the course of the night, they seem to sleep less soundly and struggle to fall back asleep, even with assistance.

Finally, keep in mind that because a baby's sleep cycles are so short, they transition frequently throughout the night, meaning an increased number of possible nocturnal arousals during which they will seek help to go back to sleep. Since babies spend more time in light sleep during the first few months of life than they do as older children and adults, they are easily aroused. If baby wakes but knows how to fall back asleep on their own, they can quickly and easily do this with minimal disruption to their own and to their parents' sleep.

All this leads to the question: When is the ideal age to start sleep training?

Between nine and twelve weeks of age, nighttime melatonin production increases substantially,[5] meaning that that sometime around the third month of life (counting from a child's estimated due date if they were born prematurely), their body starts to regularly secrete melatonin. Since melatonin is also found in breast milk,[6] nursing babies often show increased levels if they are being nursed around bedtime and throughout the night. That means that while the body is able to regulate day and night sleep from birth,[7] its ability to regulate the circadian melatonin rhythm appears closer to month three.

One truly wonderful thing about having worked through the sleep training process with hundreds of families is that I

---

5 David J. Kennaway, Frans C. Goble, and Georgina E. Stamp, "Factors Influencing the Development of Melatonin Rhythmicity in Humans," *The Journal of Clinical Endocrinology & Metabolism* 81(4) (1996): 1525-1532, doi:10.1210/jcem.81.4.8636362.

6 Helena Illnerová, Milena Buresová, and Jiri Presl, "Melatonin Rhythm in Human Milk," *The Journal of Clinical Endocrinology & Metabolism* 77(3) (1993): 838-841, doi:10.1210/jcem.77.3.8370707.

7 Andrea Attanasio, Klaus Rager, and Derek Gupta, "Ontogeny of Circadian Rhythmicity for Melatonin, Serotonin, and N-Acetylserotonin in Humans," *The Journal of Pineal Research* 3(3) (1986): 251-56, doi:10.1111/j.1600-079X.1986.tb00747.x.

get to combine my scientific knowledge with day-to-day, hands-on experience. While it's true that babies around three months of age are able to regulate their circadian rhythms and melatonin production, which would support sleep training as early as three months, I would argue that the data also bears out the fact that each baby is different, with a range of time during which they reach these milestones. While some full-term infants may be capable of regulating their sleep at nine weeks, many others do not reach readiness until closer to sixteen.[8] And because the only way to know if a particular baby is physically "ready" to sleep train is by measuring their melatonin output through their urine, I suggest all families wait until about sixteen weeks (from a baby's estimated due date) to begin sleep training.

Also, keep in mind that from month four to month six, many babies are still transitioning into the more mature REM/NREM sleep cycles. This doesn't mean that four-month-olds shouldn't be sleep trained, just that many babies under six months may struggle more with short naps, since their brains are still working out how to consistently regulate their sleep stages. While short naps in the first six months of life are the norm, rather than the exception, the vast benefits of forming healthy sleep habits as early as possible outweigh the need to wait until six months in order to begin sleep training.

---

8 David J. Kennaway, Frans C. Goble, and Georgina E. Stamp, "Factors Influencing the Development of Melatonin Rhythmicity in Humans," *The Journal of Clinical Endocrinology & Metabolism* 81(4) (1996): 1525-1532, doi:10.1210/jcem.81.4.8636362.

BEDROOM ENVIRONMENT

BEFORE GETTING INTO the techniques that will help your child get the sleep they need as quickly as possible—with the least number of tears as possible—let's discuss the importance of an appropriate sleep environment.

One common mistake parents make is not ensuring that they have their child's bedroom ready before sleep training begins. Implementing these simple recommendations can even aid in achieving better-quality sleep from birth. While they aren't a magic bullet to solve night wakings and short naps, having a sleep-conducive environment will ensure that once your child *does* learn to fall asleep unassisted, their sleep will last longer and be of better, more restorative quality.

The American Academy of Pediatrics recommends that parents room-share with their infants until at least six months, and ideally through the first year of life.[9] Despite

<hr>

9 American Academy of Pediatrics, "SIDS and Other Sleep-Related Infant Deaths: Updated 2016 Recommendations for a Safe Infant Sleeping Environment," *Pediatrics* 138(5) (2016): 1-12,

this recommendation, many families decide to move their baby into their own room as early as a few weeks of age, others closer to four, six, or twelve months. Often, parents report that sleep training is easier on both mother and baby if baby sleeps in a separate room. Seek approval from your pediatrician if your baby is under twelve months and you want to have them sleep in a separate bedroom.

Whether you decide to room share or not, the same four elements should be present in any bedroom in which a baby is sleeping. First, ensure that baby's room is as dark as possible, not just at night, but early in the morning and during naps as well. Light, especially sunlight, affects our circadian rhythms more than any other signal the body uses to regulate its internal clock. Sunlight reacts with photosensitive ganglion cells within the retina,[10] which sends the brain a message that it's time to wake up and start the day. Especially in the early morning hours, when baby is spending so much of each sleep cycle in light stage sleep, the last thing parents want is sunlight filtering in at 5:30 a.m. to wake them up (especially when they may have stayed asleep for another hour or two if the room had been darker). Darkness during naps also helps the body get more restorative, longer lasting sleep. Not to worry:

doi:10.1542/peds.2016-2938.

10 Samer Hattar, Hsi-Wen Liao, Motoharu Takao, David M. Berson, and King-Wai Yau, "Melanopsin-Containing Retinal Ganglion Cells: Architecture, Projections, and Intrinsic Photosensitivity," *Science* 295(5557) (2002): 1065-70, doi:10.1126/science.1069609.

keeping the nursery dark during naps will not cause the baby to have day/night confusion, which usually resolves on its own in the first few weeks of a baby's life. Parents should aim to cover all windows and turn off or cover any sources of artificial light (like little lights on monitors or fans). If light is filtering in through the sides of the drapes, try adhering Velcro to the wall and curtain to seal it as tightly as possible. When entering the room to check on or attend to baby, make sure the hallway light is off, so as to not introduce bright light. A good rule of thumb is that the room should be dark enough that even at noon you couldn't easily read the words on this page. At night, consider using a lamp with a fifteen-watt light bulb, turned on only when necessary during feedings or diaper changes. Red light has the fewest negative effects on sleep, so a dim red bulb is your best choice for nighttime tasks.

Second, use true white noise during all naps and throughout the night, avoiding stuffed animals that turn off after a certain interval and any noise that has detectable beats or loops. A white noise machine that produces a constant fan-like sound, or simply using a loud fan facing the wall, will help baby get to sleep faster and remain asleep longer. Our brains continue to process sounds even during sleep,[11] and especially when going between sleep cycles

11 Chiara M. Portas, Karsten Krakow, Phillip Allen, Oliver Josephs, Jorge L. Armony, and Chris D. Frith, "Auditory Processing Across the Sleep-Wake Cycle," *Neuron* 28(3) (2000): 991-99, doi:10.1016/ S0896-6273(00)00169-0.

(when sleep is very, very light). Ambient sounds can lift us completely out of the sleep state and into the wakeful state. White noise engages the brain's attention but doesn't cause it to wake up, helping it tune out any distracting sounds.[12] An adult can usually put herself back to sleep fairly easily when woken by a loud sound, but babies are often resistant to going back to sleep, especially in the early morning. Finally, white noise has been shown to reduce the complexity of brain waves,[13] prompting the brain to fall more quickly into longer periods of stable sleep.

Third, video monitors are absolutely imperative. In the coming chapters, it will become clear why being able to monitor your child's precise moments of sleep and waking is essential to getting through sleep training as painlessly as possible. In addition, video monitors can help identify potential dangers without having to be in the room with baby at all times. For example, an infant or child may pull up the fitted mattress sheet and get stuck in it. If parents are unable to visually monitor their baby at all times, they should not undertake any type of sleep training whatsoever.

---

12 Michael L. Stanchina, Muhanned Abu-Hijleh, Bilal K. Chaudhry, Carol C. Carlisle, and Richard P. Millman, "The Influence of White Noise on Sleep in Subjects Exposed to ICU Noise," *Sleep Medicine* 6(5) (2005): 423-28, doi:10.1016/j.sleep.2004.12.004.

13 Junhong Zhou, Dongdong Liu, Xin Li, Jing Ma, Jue Zhang, and Jing Fang, "Pink Noise: Effect on Complexity Synchronization of Brain Activity and Sleep Consolidation," *Journal of Theoretical Biology* 306 (2012): 68-72, doi:10.1016/j.jtbi.2012.04.006.

Parents should also ensure that they not make the common mistake of placing a video camera (or white noise machine, for that matter) in or on the crib. Many families place a camera on the crib ledge so they can get a clear view, but anything on a crib may fall and injure baby. Cameras should be mounted on the wall or placed on furniture away from the crib, also ensuring that there are no wires or cords within baby's reach. As babies grow older, so does their reach and dexterity, so cameras and other objects should be kept fully out of their reach.

Finally, a safe crib or playpen-style (PPS) portable crib is essential for babies until they reach an age where they begin to attempt to climb out, normally around eighteen months, up to four years old. A crib or PPS should have a fully flat mattress with no inclinations or elevations. Many parents are advised to raise one end of the crib or mattress to alleviate symptoms of reflux, but this can very easily cause a baby down to roll to the other end and become trapped, even with *very* slight inclinations. Inside the crib should be the snugly fitting mattress, a very-tightly-fitted sheet, and the baby. The only other acceptable items are a mesh bumper, a single lovey that is twelve inches square or smaller, and a pacifier. (Note that pacis are only okay if a baby can easily put it back into their mouth on their own, and you must get pediatrician approval first to put your baby to sleep with a pacifier in the first twelve months of life.) No other toys, blankets, bumpers, pillows, rice inside tube socks, and *especially* no inserts or sleep positioners should be inside the crib. If a parent believes baby requires a blanket, a wearable sleep sack should be used instead. There is zero benefit to any child under twelve months having pillows or plush bumpers within the crib, and if a child bumps their head into crib slats, parents should purchase individual crib slat covers, or have baby sleep in a playpen with mesh sides. Mobiles are not technically off-limits, but often provide little benefit to babies after a few months, and can be a distraction for older babies who are trying to fall asleep.

These four elements of darkness, white noise, a monitoring device, and a safe crib are all babies need in order to enjoy healthy sleep throughout their infancy and toddlerhood.

Bedroom Environment ☑

A darkened room

White noise

Video monitor

A safe crib or PPS

Optional — a single 12" lovey or pacifier*

Pacifiers should only be used during sleep training if baby can easily put the pacifier back into their mouth on their own, and you must get pediatrician approval first to put your baby to sleep without a pacifier in the first 12 months of life.

THE ELEPHANT IN THE ROOM: CRYING

YEARS AGO, WHEN I was devouring sleep-training books trying to decipher my infant daughter's sleep issues, I wondered why all the information out there seemed to be at once completely contradictory, yet strangely similar. It wasn't until a few years later, after I started working with clients, that I had an epiphany. A new mother had asked me whether or not her child would cry during sleep training, and, if so, how much. "Literally every form of sleep training is Cry It Out," I blurted out.

Different experts may use euphemistic terms to describe the process, but, at its core, every type of sleep training involves putting your child down awake and waiting for them to fall asleep on their own. Where methods differ is how parents deal with the inevitable tears when their child protests falling asleep without the help that they're used to. You may sit in a chair next to the crib, you may pick your baby up when they cry and put them down once they calm down, or you may shut the door and not return until the morning (for the record, this is not a method that I recommend), but if you read between the lines, you will see that every approach involves crying, fussing, or protesting of some sort until the child falls asleep independently. Your child *will* be unhappy about the fact that they must fall asleep in a different way to that which they are accustomed, and they will express that frustration and dissatisfaction by crying.

The reason I'm dedicating a whole chapter to crying is because I find it to be the single biggest impediment to parents pursuing, and successfully completing, sleep training. Families will endure what amounts to torture over months and years of fractured sleep, inadequate naps, and breakdowns that spring from sheer exhaustion, just to avoid those dreaded tears.

I run into two reasons that caregivers struggle with crying, the first in pretty much all families, and the second among a smaller subset.

The primary reason that parents are resistant to the crying that comes with sleep training is simply because it *feels* so wrong. This has a scientific basis. First, when babies are unhappy or frustrated, they technically scream more than cry. Studies show that we perceive screams as having a particular *roughness,* meaning that the sound of screaming itself occurs within a certain acoustic space, or level.[14] The

---

14 Luc H. Arnal, Adeen Flinker, Andreas Kleinschmidt, Anne-Lise
    Giraud, and David Poeppel, "Human Screams Occupy a Privileged
    Niche in the Communication Soundscape," *Current Biology* 25(15)

brain detects this unique quality and distinguishes it from other human sounds, like speech, triggering a fear reaction.

Second, mothers often struggle with crying more deeply than fathers (although I do get dads who hate hearing their baby cry even more than their female partner does). A new mother's amygdala—the part of the brain responsible for memory and decision-making—increases in activity, driving her to be extremely sensitive to her baby's needs, and related hormones generate positive feelings when she takes care of her baby. This hormonal reward system feels good and keeps mothers doting and caring. This more active amygdala also encourages Mom to bond with her baby over all others. During pregnancy and after birth, mothers experience an enormous increase in the "love hormone" oxytocin while looking at, nursing, or cuddling their babies. To understand how a flood of oxytocin feels, think back to the first time you feel head-over-heels for someone.

So here you have a mother who is *incredibly* bonded to her baby: biologically driven to ensure their survival, with a deep emotional connection. Quite literally, she is enamored, and likely feels a love for her child that she has never experienced before. Her brain has undergone an enormous shift, one that may be permanent.[15] Now she

(2015): 2051-56, doi:10.1016/j.cub.2015.06.043.

15 Elseline Hoekzema, Erika Barba-Müller, Cristina Pozzobon, Marisol Picado, Florencio Lucco, David García-García, Juan Carlos

hears her baby crying. Beyond driving her to care for her baby, some scientists believe that increased oxytocin also elevates her ability to distinguish their cries. Recall that a baby's cry registers as a scream, prompting a fear response: cold sweat, anxiety, and increased heartbeat. If she is unable to stop the tears, she can feel impotent and neglectful.

I also see families that want to prevent their baby from crying because of a widespread pseudoscientific myth about cortisol and sleep training. Before we go further, let's talk about how cortisol works. Cortisol is a hormone that regulates glucose and aids the body in reducing inflammation. As part of our hormonal regulatory systems, everybody releases cortisol throughout the day and night, with increases during, for example, a sickness (activating the immune system and/or the anti-inflammatory response). The body will also release surges of cortisol in response to anything perceived as stressful. Somewhere along the line, supposed experts started to suggest that *any* time a child has elevated cortisol levels, it might be harmful in and of itself, perhaps because the body releases more of it in stressful situations. However, the mere *presence* of cortisol does not indicate stress, nor does the occasional surge of cortisol mean that the body or brain are undergoing permanent damage. Humans release cortisol all day long

Soliva, Adolf Tobeña, Manuel Desco, Eveline A. Crone, Agustín Ballesteros, Susanna Carmona, and Oscar Vilarroya, "Pregnancy Leads to Long-Lasting Changes in Human Brain Structure," *Nature Neuroscience* 20(2) (2017): 287-300, doi:10.1038/nn.4458.

to deal with the variety of normal stressors. Once a stressful event passes, cortisol returns to its normal levels.

Only when cortisol stays abnormally high for extended periods of time, or when it is greatly diminished, do we need to worry. Chronic stress, such as seen in children who experience abuse or who, ironically, are extremely sleep deprived over months or years, causes the adrenal system (responsible for releasing cortisol) to burn out, which is known as adrenal fatigue. The adrenals are then unable to produce adequate amounts of cortisol, decreasing the immune system's ability to fight illness, triggering an imbalance in blood sugar and problems with thyroid regulation, and leading to sleep issues.

And that brings us back to sleep training. When done responsibly, sleep training, at worst, creates a temporary bump in cortisol levels. There are some who claim that scientific evidence proves that the crying associated with sleep training harms children. I've read those studies, and they have absolutely nothing to do with the type of sleep training recommended in this book (in one oft-cited study, the subjects were neglected children in orphanages).[16] Research on sleep training in families with healthy

---

16 Matthew Malter Cohena, Deqiang Jingb, Rui R. Yangb, Nim Tottenhama, Francis S. Leeb, and B. J. Caseya, "Early-Life Stress has Persistent Effects on Amygdala Function and Development in Mice and Humans," *Proceedings of the National Academy of Sciences of the United States of America* 110(45) (2013): 18274–78, doi:10.1073/pnas.1310163110.

attachments consistently shows that it causes no emotional damage in the immediate, short, or long term.[17][18] Studies also consistently show that one thing that *definitely* causes long-term harm is chronic sleep deprivation.

It is helpful for parents to keep in mind that babies or toddlers may experience frustration, tiredness, or stress during sleep training. I've had many families ask me if their child's behavior was something to worry about; some simply act more tired or fussy, sometimes even seeming a bit withdrawn as they go through the process of learning to fall asleep unassisted. I always refer parents to their pediatrician, who have in every case confirmed that whatever behaviors the child displays while going through sleep training are temporary and due to the effort of learning a new skill.

On a purely anecdotal note, I have never once had a family return to tell me that their child had a permanent shift in their personality or behavior due to sleep training. Even in the very rare instances where parents decided sleep

17 Anna M.H. Price, Melissa Wake, Obioha C. Ukoumunne, and Harriet Hiscock, "Five-Year Follow-up of Harms and Benefits of Behavioral Infant Sleep Intervention: Randomized Trial," *Pediatrics* 130(4) (2012): 643-51, doi:10.1542/peds.2011-3467.

18 Michael Gradisar, Kate Jackson, Nicola J. Spurrier, Joyce Gibson, Justine Whitham, Anne Sved Williams, Robyn Dolby, and David J. Kennaway, "Behavioral Interventions for Infant Sleep Problems: A Randomized Controlled Trial," *Pediatrics* 137(6): 1-10, doi:10.1542/peds.2015-1486.

training was not for them for one reason or another, none have ever indicated to me that their child had a negative change in personality. To the contrary, reports of children being happier, healthier, and *less* fussy abound. Also, keep in mind that babies often cry for extended periods in the car seat or when starting daycare, or if they have to go to the hospital due to a serious illness or injury. Most parents don't worry that their child will be permanently damaged by these temporarily stressful experiences.

There will always be those who vociferously oppose parents who allow their babies to cry during sleep training. I suspect I will hear from many of them directly via e-mail and online review portals. Nonetheless, crying for the purposes of sleep training does not harm children in any way. If a parent has discussed their sleep training plan with their pediatrician, is meeting all of their child's physical and emotional needs, is checking on them repeatedly throughout the process, and is immediately addressing any emergent issues, sleep training will only serve to help baby and family thrive.

NEWBORN SLEEP

I WISH I could banish the term "trying not to create bad habits" from the modern parent's vernacular—there's enough pressure on them as it is! Even for an expert like me, sleep training a newborn is *hard* (in many cases, impossible), and the truth is, it's not necessary in the first sixteen weeks. As long as a newborn is happy and healthy, my advice is that parents not pursue sleep training until their child is at least sixteen weeks old, counting from their estimated due date. But there is a lot you can do to *encourage* your newborn to sleep as well as they are able to, hopefully resulting in longer stretches of sleep for baby and parents.

In 1992, the American Academy of Pediatrics released their recommendation that infants from birth to twelve months sleep only on their backs, significantly reducing the number of infant deaths classified as SIDS (Sudden Infant Death Syndrome). However, this wonderful and life-saving recommendation had an unexpected side effect: now, baby needed help to fall asleep. Previously, parents had usually been advised to put baby to sleep on their stomach, which, due to what's called the Moro reflex, usually results in newborns rousing less frequently, getting longer stretches of uninterrupted sleep, and falling back to sleep more easily without assistance. Let's be clear: a newborn may sleep more easily on their stomach, but *all babies should always be put to sleep on their backs through the twelfth month of life.* No amount of sleep is worth the very real risk of suffocation from stomach sleeping.

Since virtually all babies are now placed on their backs to sleep, parents quickly find that they must help them fall asleep for naps and at bedtime, throughout the night, and sometimes in the middle of a nap. Techniques might include a tight swaddle, a specially designed sleep rocker, and co-sleeping, all which will be discussed in more detail in this chapter. Since it is totally developmentally appropriate for newborn babies to develop a dependence on some form of assistance to fall asleep (just like it's developmentally appropriate for young children to use training wheels on their bicycles), parents should not waste any time trying to avoid "bad habits." In the overwhelming majority of cases, it will be impossible for newborns to keep from developing a dependence on whatever form of assistance they need in order to fall asleep; likewise, nearly all babies will need to break that dependence at some point, which is when we begin sleep training.

It should also be noted that some newborns can sleep for what may seem like an incredibly long time—up to eighteen to twenty hours per day! Most newborn sleep is REM sleep (during which dreaming takes place), and as they grow, their sleep cycles become more regular. As a child approaches four months and their sleep cycles become increasingly more adult-like, parents often notice an uptick in nocturnal arousals and an increased difficulty in getting them back to sleep. The older a baby is and the more aware they are, the more likely they are to fight falling asleep and require more help, whether via rocking, feeding, etc.

So, what *can* you do to not only help your newborn get the sleep they need, but also lay a solid foundation for future sleep?

1. Focus on figuring out how your newborn likes to sleep. As long as they are not able to flip over, swaddling is generally considered safe, although you should always check with your pediatrician to make sure they recommend it for your child. When learning how your newborn prefers to be soothed (whether it's bouncing on a yoga ball, being taken into a dark room with loud white noise for a break from any commotion, or hanging out in a swiftly moving swing or bouncer), it is wise to try and avoid relying on feeding. Of course, in the early weeks it will be next to impossible to keep your baby awake while feeding; however, as time goes on, it will be easier and easier to help them fall asleep in other ways. Feeding-to-sleep can be tricky to extricate yourself from, so it's often better to

avoid from the start. Please note, if your child is sleeping anywhere *other* than an empty crib, they should be within your direct line of sight at all times. Under no circumstances should a baby of any age be allowed to sleep unsupervised in anything other than an empty crib.

2. Make sure that as they move past the sixth week of life (when newborns seem to suddenly rouse from sleep and are not as apt to fall asleep anywhere and everywhere like they used to), you begin to put them to sleep for both naps and at nighttime in a very dark room with loud white noise. The white noise machine should make a constant whirring sound—avoid sounds like the ocean, rain, and lullabies. When considering volume, remember that babies in the womb are exposed to constant sound, as loud as a lawnmower! As long as your white noise machine isn't deafening, consider it safe for your baby's ears.

3. The American Academy of Pediatrics recommends room sharing (but *not* bed sharing) from birth through at least the sixth, but preferably the twelfth, month of life. If you find yourself wanting to put your newborn in their own room, check first with your medical provider.

4. Ensure that *wherever* baby is sleeping, safety is your utmost concern. Cribs should be completely flat, with no bumpers, pillows, blankets, or any other

objects inside. Small lovies, less than twelve inches square, are technically safe, but are unnecessary for newborns. Likewise, mesh bumpers are considered safe, but are unnecessary in the first weeks of life. Sleep-sack-style wearable blankets are a great idea if a parent is concerned their child might be cold at bedtime.

5. If a baby takes naps or sleeps at night away from their parent or caretaker, a video monitor should be on them at all times, and they should only be put to sleep in a room other than their parents' bedroom with direct pediatrician approval.

Where your newborn sleeps is just as important as how they fall asleep. The safest place is a flat, empty crib or Pack-n'-Play-style portable crib in your bedroom. Side-car-style baby sleepers that pull right up to the side of the parents' bed are also a safe option when used as instructed. Although many parents find that their babies sleep well in co-sleepers, swings, "nests" to be used in beds, bassinets, and rockers, the general consensus is that these are not safe when used without direct supervision; in certain circumstances, however, parents may find that their pediatrician approves their use.

Parents may think that elevating the crib mattress to relieve symptoms of reflux is safe, but it is not, nor are any types of sleep positioners or wedges in a crib. Furthermore, however safe the crib may be, any new parent can attest to the fact that all babies will end up sleeping in many other places. Make sure that if your infant is falling asleep in a stroller, car seat, swing, or bouncer, swaddled or not, they are always within eyesight and earshot. Each year, babies die from asphyxiation when their chins tuck too closely to their chest from a seated position in their car seat. The same goes for any type of wrap or carrier—always be vigilant about making sure your baby is able to breathe easily. Finally, avoid sleeping with your infant on a couch or chair, as easy and tempting as it may be. Especially when you are sleep deprived, it's important that every precaution is taken to make sure baby is never in an unsafe position at a moment when you may fall so deeply asleep that you don't notice.

Co-Sleeping

The AAP states that "bed sharing remains the greatest risk factor for sleep related infant deaths," and recommends *room* sharing instead.[19] However, since many parents will find themselves sharing a bed with their baby at some point, it is vital that safe co-sleeping practices are undertaken. Recently, the AAP did release some general guidelines, and there are several specific, common-sense practices that can

19 American Academy of Pediatrics, "Bed Sharing Remains Greatest Risk Factor for Sleep Related Infant Deaths," press release, July 14, 2014, https://www.aap.org/en-us/about-the-aap/aap-press-room/pages/bed-sharing-remains-greatest-risk-factor-for-sleep-related-infant-deaths.aspx.

also be followed to ensure that you and your newborn are co-sleeping safely.

1. Parents should make sure that baby is sleeping on their back and that the mattress is very firm, avoiding memory-foam-style mattresses.

2. The mattress should fit properly within the bed frame, avoiding any large gaps into which baby might slip (this is, sadly, not uncommon, and has happened to two families I know).

3. All bedding should be fitted snugly to the mattress, and there should be *no* loose blankets or pillows near the baby.

4. In addition, it's important that the adult(s) sharing the bed with baby never be under the influence of drugs, alcohol, or any other substances that might cause them to sleep unnaturally deeply.

5. Siblings should not share a bed with an infant under the age of one.

6. Infants should not be swaddled while bed sharing.

7. Very long hair should be secured, since long strands can wrap around a baby's neck.

In the early days and weeks of a baby's life, most families will find that their child seems to sleep quite a bit. There may be long wakeful periods, or day/night confusion, when the baby is awake at night and sleeps the day away. It may be helpful to think of the newborn period as distinct stages, each with particular characteristics. When counting weeks during the newborn stages, parents should count week one from the baby's *estimated* due date, not the baby's actual birth date, if it was prior to the fortieth week of pregnancy.

Early Newborn Stage: Birth through Week Six

During this stage, parents will find that for the most part their babies sleep anywhere, especially while on the go or being held. In rare cases, very young newborns will cry fitfully, and this is generally a sign of either digestive distress or a feeding issue, like not yet getting enough breast milk. Any severe crying during this stage should be brought to the attention of your pediatrician.

In the first six weeks, parents should focus on establishing the feeding relationship, whether via breast or bottle/formula feeding. Mom should simply focus on recuperating and enjoying her new baby. If any feeding issues arise, especially for breastfeeding mothers, they should be addressed straight away with the help of a lactation consultant. While a few popular sleep books advocate some form of sleep training starting within the first twelve weeks of life, results are inconsistent, and the stress for both the parents and child is not worth an uncertain outcome.

If parents are interested, they can begin to establish practices such as swaddling, white noise, and using a pacifier to help soothe their fussy baby. If possible, parents should make sure that their baby does not sleep longer than two hours at a single stretch between about 7:00 a.m. to 9:00 p.m.—anything after that can be considered nighttime sleep. When waking baby from a long nap, aim to keep them awake for thirty to fifty minutes (including feeding time), and then nap again. Limiting the lengths of naps to no more than two hours in the early days and weeks is the single best thing parents can do to resolve day/night confusion quickly and to encourage baby to have longer stretches of overnight sleep.

Late Newborn Stage: Week Six through Week 16

This can be particularly challenging time. Around week six is typically when babies become much more alert, and reflux issues often emerge. Your formerly peaceful and calm baby may now become fussy, even inconsolable, especially around dinnertime—the newborn witching hour.

It is around this age when parents can try in earnest to establish healthy sleep habits. Whenever baby is sleeping at home, the room should be very dark, with loud white noise. Unless co-sleeping is a strong preference, parents can try to make sleeping in a crib, Pack 'n Play, or side-car co-sleeper a priority, making sure to swaddle baby snugly (until baby can roll over; then swaddling should be stopped immediately).

Parents can begin to establish a "start" time each day to wake baby up. Ideally, this would be more or less the same time each morning, but it can vary by about thirty to sixty minutes. Regardless of when baby wakes, parents should begin to instill a cycle of eating, being awake, and falling asleep. This cycle may be established in the Early Newborn Stage, but will be easier to do once the baby is slightly more awake and aware after week six. After establishing a start time to each day and ensuring that baby does not nap longer than two hours for any single nap, the most important thing parents can focus on is making sure baby stays as awake as possible during feeding time. At first, for a baby who is used to eating and sleeping simultaneously, try one feeding each day during which baby is fed immediately upon waking. Parents can help baby stay awake by undressing them, rubbing a cool washcloth over their forehead, or changing their diaper midway through feeding. Even if baby does fall asleep or doze, they should be woken immediately after the feeding is finished, and kept awake until they show a sleep cue. This wakeful period can last anywhere from thirty to ninety minutes, depending on the baby and time of day. Then, baby should be helped to fall asleep in any way that does not involve feeding (if possible).

Generally speaking, newborns have shorter intervals earlier in the day during which they are comfortably awake before needing to nap, and extend their periods of being happily awake towards the end of the day. To recognize their baby's sleep cues (keeping in mind that a small percentage of babies seem to show no sleep cues at all), parents should start to closely observe baby thirty to forty minutes after they wake. Typical signs a baby is ready to sleep include eye rubbing, fussiness, sudden disengagement with whatever they were doing, yawning, or staring. Sleep cues can vary widely, but most parents can learn to identity them after careful observation.

As soon as they notice a sleep cue, a parent should immediately swaddle baby and, if possible, take them to a dark room with loud white noise. At this point, anything *but* feeding should be used to try to help baby sleep. Rocking, swaying, shushing, bouncing on a yoga ball, using a pacifier, etc., are all great approaches. With direct one-on-one supervision (and pediatrician approval), baby can also sleep in a swing or rocker. After a baby falls asleep and wakes again, they should be fed, even if their previous feeding was less than two hours prior. The idea that a newborn should only be fed every three to four hours during the day in order to extend nighttime sleep does not usually result in extended night sleep. Instead, it's simply the regular *cycle* of eating, being awake, sleeping, then eating again that helps the body sleep for longer stretches at night. Establishing this cycle ensures that babies have frequent opportunities to eat throughout the day and encourages less waking at night. Formula-fed babies may not be ready to eat right after waking, especially after a short nap, so parents can wait and attempt a feeding again after about fifteen to thirty minutes, ensuring baby stays awake the entire feeding.

Contrary to popular wisdom, an elaborate bedtime routine is not necessary for quality nighttime sleep. In fact, a brief routine is all that babies need to learn to recognize sleep times. Parents should feed baby in a well-lit room about a half-hour before bedtime (which can be as late as 11:00 p.m. for newborns or as early as 6:00 p.m. for three-month-olds), making sure to keep baby as fully awake as possible, and should then proceed with pajamas and swaddling, or a bath. Darkness, white noise, and the baby's own body will be the best prompts to help baby know that it's time to go to sleep.

As we've established, what happens during the day has a direct impact on how well a newborn sleeps at night. However, certain evening practices can also help baby sleep more soundly overnight. Unless absolutely necessary, parents should avoid changing their baby's diaper and/or unswaddling them from bedtime (whatever time parents deem to that be) until morning. If a diaper must be changed, it should be done either when switching from one breast to the next or halfway through baby finishing bottle. Also, parents should make sure to use low (fifteen watts and under) or no lighting at night.

What is Dreamfeeding?

Dreamfeeding can buy parents an extra hour or two of nighttime sleep, or at the very least get more calories into baby in each twenty-four-hour period. Generally speaking, dreamfeeding should be limited to babies who are swaddled and younger than sixteen weeks. In order to dreamfeed properly, a parent or caretaker should enter the room sometime between 9:30 and 11:30 p.m., gently scoop up the swaddled baby, and either immediately begin feeding, or hand baby to the nursing parent. Baby's eyes should remain closed throughout the entire feeding in order for the dreamfeed not to be disruptive to the rest of nighttime sleep. If baby rouses during feeding, that is okay, but as soon as a parent suspects that the dreamfeed is disrupting their child's sleep, it should be stopped. If baby refuses to open their mouth because they are just too tired, that's okay! Some babies need to try dreamfeeding a few times before its sticks. Parents should attempt to burp baby after the dreamfeed, but shouldn't necessarily be concerned if baby doesn't respond with a burp. Melatonin, the hormone responsible for making a person feel tired and for relaxing the smooth muscle groups (namely the arms, legs, and abdominal muscles), is widespread in the body at bedtime and for several hours afterwards.[20] Relaxed abdominal muscles often result in less or no spitting up since there's little pressure on the stomach. After a dreamfeed, feedings should continue throughout the night as often

---

20 Maria J. Pozo, Pedro J. Gomez-Pinilla, Cristina Camello-Almaraz, Francisco E. Martin-Cano, Patricia Pascua, Maria Angeles Rol, Dario Acuna-Castroviejo, Pedro J. Camello, "Melatonin, A Potential Therapeutic Agent for Smooth Muscle-Related Pathological Conditions and Aging," *Current Medical Chemistry* 17(34) (2010): 4150-65, doi:10.2174/092986710793348536.

as baby wakes hungry. With pediatrician permission, it is acceptable to wait three to five minutes after baby wakes to see if a they are truly awake and hungry, or simply making sounds as they transition from one sleep cycle to the next.

I've laid out some of the ways you can start encouraging healthy sleep hygiene, but don't worry about starting official sleep training in the first four months of your baby's life. Your newborn is dealing with a lot, from digestive issues to learning how to regulate their breathing and temperature. The most important thing to keep in mind is that no matter what a parent does, as long as they are loving and caring for their child and themselves, they are doing everything right! The newborn stage can be both very exciting and very trying, and parents should simply focus on doing the best they can to help their child thrive.

Newborn "Cheat Sheet" for Creating Positive Sleep Habits: ☑

Master the swaddle and other soothing techniques

Naps in darkened rooms with loud white noise

Room share not bed share*

Make sure their crib or PPS is absolutely safe!

Always video monitor your baby if they are in another room

EXTRA CREDIT (0-6 weeks)

Limit any single nap to no longer than 2 hours (between 7am and 9pm)

Aim to keep baby awake for no longer than 30-50 minutes (including feeding time) between naps

EXTRA CREDIT (6 weeks+)

Establish a start time to each day

Instill the wake & eat, stay awake & play, fall asleep again cycle

Try to help baby stay awake during feedings

Learn baby's sleep cues and put them to sleep when you see one! (preferably without a feeding)

Begin a simple, short bedtime routine

*Unless your pediatrician has given you permission to move them to their own room

NIGHTTIME SLEEP TRAINING

OKAY, LET'S GET started! My method, which will help your baby learn to calmly fall asleep at bedtime and return to sleep easily throughout the night, can be used with infants as young as four months. It can also be used with children until they are no longer in a crib, which is hopefully sometime between three and four years, although some children as young as seventeen months (or younger!) can climb out of their cribs and should be moved to a toddler bed immediately. Remember to consult your pediatrician before embarking on sleep training.

If you get overwhelmed, remember that you have everything you need to be totally successful with nighttime training in your hands, and that as long as you start sleep training at bedtime and nap training the next day, your child will quickly learn to sleep healthfully. The first forty-eight hours will be the most intense, so it is especially important you embark on your sleep-training journey prepared to commit 100 percent for two days. The rest of the training period will be much easier and move along a lot more quickly.

When is it time to move my child from a crib to a bed?

In my extensive experience, I have found that it is extremely wise to keep your child in a crib *as long as humanly possible*. It is the rare case when the move to a bed does not result in some sort of major sleep regression. The younger the child is, the more likely they are to use their newfound freedom to leave their bedroom instead of staying in bed and going to sleep. As long as your pediatrician approves, keeping your child in their crib through age three or four will go a long way in ensuring solid nighttime and nap sleep. It is ideal to transition children from cribs to beds only once they are old enough to understand that they must stay in their bed or their room until a predetermined time each morning.

It is not uncommon for a two-year-old to go through a stage of light sleep at 5:30 a.m., and, if they are still in a comfortable and familiar crib, to lie there quietly until they go back to sleep. If that same two-year-old is sleeping a toddler bed, they are more likely to realize that they'd rather get up and play with toys, wake a sibling, or come into their parents' room instead of going back to sleep. In the crib, it never occurred to them that getting up earlier was an option, but now they can exercise their freedom and start their day! This might also happen at bedtime or in the middle of the night, with a toddler leaving their bedroom repeatedly simply because they can. For this reason, a child should *not* be moved to a toddler bed because a new sibling needs their crib. It's preferable to put a younger sibling in their own crib than it is to take away an older child's crib and transition them to a bed.

Later on in this chapter, we'll discuss how you'll know when to transition to a bed and how to do so properly, but for the time being, know that keeping your child in a crib should be your goal until at least age three years of age.

To Feed or Not to Feed

Before starting nighttime sleep training, decide whether or not you will be feeding your baby overnight. It is patently false that it is harder to sleep train a baby who is still feeding overnight, but it is important to decide whether or not your child *needs* a nighttime feeding. If they do, then hunger will wake them, you will feed them, and they will ideally fall back asleep quickly. However, if your child does not *need* a nighttime feeding, offering them one will make it extremely difficult for them to understand why some wakings are responded to with a feeding and others are not, leading to a bad cycle of crying and more wakings.

Many babies between four and six months still need a feeding overnight, though in my non-medical experience it is rare for a baby over four months and at least thirteen to fourteen pounds to need more than one feeding per night. Babies over six months and at least fifteen to seventeen pounds rarely need an overnight feeding. Ask your pediatrician whether *your* child needs one. There's a difference between saying that *some* babies keep a feeding through the ninth month and confirming that your particular baby should. Keep in mind that just because they're used to eating overnight, or even in cases in which a baby is reverse-cycling and getting most of their calories overnight, does not mean a child needs a night feeding. Whatever you decide, it is possible to be successful with sleep training while keeping a night feed. Ideally, baby should have one only if you and your doctor determine that they are unable to consume enough calories during waking hours.

Whatever choice you make, all weaning must happen prior to beginning sleep training. For tips on how to wean off of night feedings and how to keep up your milk supply after cutting night feeds, see Troubleshooting After Sleep Training Issues at the end of this chapter.

Pediatrician Checklist

Here are some important questions to ask your pediatrician before you start training:

For children younger than one year:

- What should I do if my child flips to their belly during sleep? Should I leave them there or flip them back? If I flip them back and they continue to roll back to their belly, is there a limit to how many times or for how long I should continue to roll them back?

- How many night feeds does my child need, and at what age can I wean night feedings?

- What is the best method for night weaning?

- Is it okay for me and my child to sleep in separate bedrooms?

- Is it okay for my child to fall asleep without a pacifier? This is an important question to ask your doctor. The AAP recommends that babies under twelve months of age use a pacifier while they sleep, but that can inhibit them from learning to fall asleep unassisted.

Creating a Sleep-Smart Bedtime Routine

Once you have made sure that your child's bedroom environment is set up with the four elements discussed previously (total darkness, loud white noise at an appropriate distance, a safe crib, and a video monitor), and you have determined whether or not you are going to be keeping a night feeding, you are ready to begin sleep training. Sleep training should only begin at bedtime, never at naptime. The only thing left to decide is what time bedtime will be in your home. Most babies will respond best to a bedtime around 7:00 p.m., give or take thirty minutes. The younger the child, the earlier they will probably prefer to go to bed for the night. Only in extenuating circumstances (a parent not getting home from work until late, for example) should a child's bedtime be later than 7:30 p.m.

We will be using a one-to-ten scale to determine the optimal level of wakefulness or sleepiness at various stages of your child's bedtime and naptime routines, and throughout each day. A baby at one is totally happy, engaged, and awake! By the time they hit five, they're rubbing their eyes and yawning, and at ten, they're so deeply asleep that it is possible to pick them up and move them without waking them. From the end of your child's last nap of the day through the start of your bedtime routine, children should be kept at between one and three. That means that parents must be careful that their kids not become sleepy or drowsy in the few hours before bedtime, especially while driving or taking a walk. As a parent myself, I know how challenging it can be to keep a fussy child awake, but for the least amount of crying while your child learns to put themselves to sleep at bedtime, it's imperative they be kept fully awake in the hours before being put down to sleep. A tired baby can often be kept happily engaged by stepping outside into direct sunlight or playing in a warm bath.

The 1-10 Wakefulness Scale

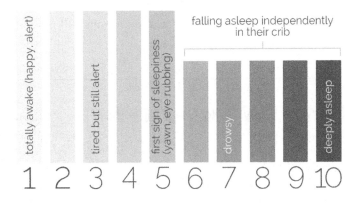

If your child is still nursing or bottle-feeding, their final feeding should occur thirty minutes before bedtime (unless feeding your baby usually takes longer than ten to fifteen minutes, in which case start about forty minutes before bedtime). This final feeding *must* be the first part of your bedtime routine. It should take place in a well-lit room, since it is imperative that throughout the feeding the child be kept between one and three on the wakefulness scale. If they become sleepy or drowsy, it can greatly impact their ability to fall asleep at bedtime. Almost falling asleep, or drowsing off completely, then being woken up and put down again is one of the most common reasons babies cry at bedtime. If you struggle to keep baby awake, stop the feeding the instant the child hits a three on the scale and help them become more alert and aware; then you may complete the feeding. Many parents have success giving the last bottle while baby is taking a bath in an infant tub in the sink, or breastfeeding while keeping the TV or music on. If your child is easily distractible, it's acceptable to feed them in a quiet room, as long as they remain 100 percent awake throughout the *entire* feeding.

What If My Child Uses a Pacifier?

If your child uses a pacifier but they are not yet dexterous enough to reach out, grab it, and insert it in their mouth, you should not give it to them after the final feeding, nor within thirty minutes of nap time (if your doctor agrees to not using it during sleep training). If you use a pacifier during sleep training when a baby is too young to insert it on their own, training will likely be unsuccessful. Here's why: If a child is accustomed to falling asleep with a pacifier and is not able to reinsert it when they wake up, they will call for help. If you don't help, you are setting them up for failure, because they will continue to wake and cry, since they need that assistance to fall asleep. If you *do* help, they are still relying on you to fall asleep, which means that you are not actually sleep training them.

Even if your child is old enough to maneuver the paci on their own, it is important to keep in mind that once they are sleep trained with it, you should plan on keeping it until they are done napping. It is not at all uncommon that if you take away a paci from a two- or three-year-old, they'll stop napping for weeks or months on end, or to give up their nap completely (since it is so much harder to sleep during the day than at night, taking it away can affect naps more catastrophically than bedtime). If you know that you'll want to get rid of the paci before age three or four, it is a good idea to say goodbye during sleep training. The younger your child, the easier it is to wean off a paci, so sleep training is a great natural point to get rid of it altogether.

Regardless of whether you keep or get rid of the paci for sleep, feel free to keep using it during other parts of the day, just not within thirty minutes of naps or bedtime.

After the final feeding, start the rest of the bedtime routine. Contrary to popular belief, it matters very little how long or short your routine is. Bottle, pajamas, and bed is sufficient, provided the four key bedroom elements discussed in the Bedroom Environment section are in place. Bedtime routines can also include a bath and books, but parents should make sure that their kids are happy and awake, not fussy and tired, before beginning a routine. A fussy baby is not helped by being forced to sit through a book when all they want to do is go to sleep. However elaborate or concise your routine is, the most important thing is keeping your child between a one and a three on the wakefulness scale.

After you have fully completed the bedtime routine, get into the habit of following this soothing procedure: Five minutes prior to your child's determined bedtime, walk into their room (if you are not already there), set a timer for five minutes on a cell phone or watch and place it in your back pocket, turn off the lights, close the door, and turn the white noise to the loudest volume you feel comfortable with. In those five minutes, do everything you can to try to help your child go from a one, two, or three to a four or five (eye rubbing, yawning, relaxing), while *avoiding* any physical movements you know will make them sleepy or drowsy. If you usually bounce or rock them a certain way to get them to fall asleep, don't make those movements during the five-minute calming time. Instead, focus on holding your child very still, walking slowly around the room, or rocking gently. Especially if they are agitated or having a hard time calming down, it's important that your energy level be soothing and low-key to give them a chance to relax. As soon as you feel them calm down or yawn (even if it's before the five minutes are up), immediately put them in the crib, give them a kiss and tell them, "It's time to go to sleep. I love you," and leave the room. If the five-minute timer goes off and your baby still has not become calm or relaxed, or even if they are fussy, put them down in the same way (kiss, "love you") and leave the room.

For many families, this will be a radical change to how things are normally done. Your child may be shifting from co-sleeping, sleeping in a swing, or being rocked or bounced or fed to sleep. No matter how they were sleeping before, it's important that this part of their bedtime routine be handled exactly as outlined above, with *no variations*, even though it may feel drastic. In my work with hundreds of children, I have learned the most humane thing families can do is to create a thoughtful plan, then execute it swiftly and consistently. It is the constant attempt to wean and approach sleep training gradually that tends to cause the most turmoil and failure. Furthermore, it is easier for a child to deal with one large change than smaller changes over longer periods of time.

Once your child is in their crib, they will likely protest the fact that you are not helping them fall asleep. Depending on their age and awareness level, this may happen immediately or after a few minutes. Whenever the crying starts, you will want to set a timer to determine when to go in for checks. Ideally, checks should be at least ten to fifteen minutes, and no longer than twenty minutes, apart. Ten minutes may feel like an eternity, especially to parents who, as we discussed, are affected physically, mentally, and emotionally by their child's cry. If it is absolutely impossible to wait ten minutes, get as close to ten as possible, and do your checks at those intervals. The older the child, the more beneficial it is for checks to be farther apart. I regularly speak with clients who tell me they've attempted checks every five or so minutes, only to have their child completely panic when they leave. It's important to give your child time to recognize what it feels like to want to go to sleep without any help. Also, do *not* begin at shorter intervals (e.g., five minutes) and "work up" to ten minutes. Your baby will not be able to fall asleep within that short amount of time, and checking in so frequently will wake them up, instead of helping them get sleepier.

It is also very, very important that a parent does not let the intensity of their child's cries determine when to do a check. If at any moment, for any reason, a parent or caretaker suspects something might be wrong, they should of course immediately go into the room to make sure the child is safe and sound. However, in almost all cases, a frustrated and angry reaction at having to fall asleep unassisted doesn't mean there is something amiss. Watching closely on the monitor and sticking to the predetermined check-in intervals will balance your need to check on baby with their need to have time to fall asleep independently.

Remember that your baby is having an experience that's

driven by equal parts biology and personality. Just like most of us have had the experience of driving late at night, willing ourselves to stay awake with caffeine, a blasting AC, and loud music, only to realize that our bodies are going to succumb to sleep whether we like it or not, babies will not be able to fight sleep indefinitely. Given the proper environment and time on their own, their bodies *are* capable of falling asleep— and will do so. As a sleep consultant, one of my pet peeves is when an anti-sleep-training advocate suggests that babies are simply crying until they're exhausted, then passing out. This is a wholly inaccurate description of how the body goes to sleep—and a misunderstanding of our biological *need* to sleep! I have never heard of a marathon runner crossing the finish line, then falling asleep instantly, nor did I go to sleep the second I gave birth to my first child, after being in full, un-medicated labor for thirteen straight hours. Bodies give into sleep when they are biologically meant to, *not* just when they have physically tired themselves out.

When it comes time to do a check, you should walk into baby's room and, if they are not yet old enough to kneel, sit or stand, go right up to them, touch them (without picking them up), and talk to them in a soothing way for about thirty seconds. You can rub baby's stomach or face, give them a kiss, or pat their chest; just make sure *not* to pick them up or stay longer than thirty seconds (regardless of whether or not they calm down). If your child is old enough to kneel, sit, or stand, it's important that you stay about three to four feet away from the crib, close enough to make eye contact and talk to baby, but not close enough that they'll anticipate getting picked up. Generally, once babies are able to stand up, check-ins that involve touching will panic them and make them much more upset once the parent leaves. In any situation, remember, the purpose of checks is not to help your child fall asleep, but to allow your child to see you so they know you are there and that you love them, and to make sure they aren't in need of a diaper change or some similar type of assistance. When you go in, make sure that light does not flood into the room from the hallway.

During these check-in intervals (around ten minutes apart), you want to be watching very closely through the monitor for either one of the following two scenarios. One is very likely to occur and is a good sign that sleep is imminent, and the other is extremely rare, happening with less than five percent of children I work with.

1. If you notice at any point during the ten-plus min-
    ute check-in interval that your child takes a break in
    crying for anything more than to catch their breath
    (three seconds or longer), and then resumes cry-
    ing, reset your timer to zero. Believe it or not, those
    breaks are the first sign your child is giving that they
    are recognizing that they feel tired and they want
    and need to go to sleep. Kids will often take a break,
    cry again, take another break, start crying again,
    etc., until they fall asleep. Even if a break in crying
    occurs at nine minutes, thirty seconds, restart your
    timer to zero—that is, only do a check-in if your
    child has been protesting without breaks for a full

ten minutes, or the length of your chosen interval. If you go in regularly and indiscriminately, your child will end up crying for longer, since your presence will bring them out of edging toward sleep (represented by those pauses in crying) and make them restart the process.

2. You'll also want to make sure that your checks are not keeping your child awake. You will know this is the case if you have done checks for about an hour straight and your child is still crying and not yet asleep. As I mentioned, this is rare; however, some children find the check-ins disruptive instead of helping them get closer to sleep. If it has been an hour and your child is still awake, you will want to stop checking in altogether, observe your child through the monitor, and allow them to take all the time they need to fall asleep on their own, which almost always occurs relatively quickly once the check-ins stop. Resume checks, or feed baby, if necessary, for all subsequent wakings that occur before 4:00 a.m. Remember that when your baby wakes throughout the night, you should first wait the full length of your interval before doing a check, instead of going in the moment you hear them wake up.

If you're not feeding your child overnight, resume check-ins (starting the timer at every waking, waiting the full length of your interval before doing a check, re-starting the timer to zero once you detect a pause in crying, and not doing checks for more than an hour before allowing baby to fall asleep on their own) each time they wake until 4:00 a.m.

If your child is going to keep an overnight feeding, aim for it to take place the first time they wake after about 1:00 a.m. (as long as your pediatrician approves waiting to feed until then). Since the brain spends almost the entirety of each sleep cycle in deep sleep during the first half of the night, it's unlikely that prior wakings are due to hunger. It's much more difficult for a baby to go without eating from about 10:00 p.m. to 7:00 a.m. than for them to go to bed at 7:00 p.m. and wake for a feeding around 2:00 a.m. Ideally, you want the gap between morning wake-up and their night feeding to be shorter rather than longer. If you and your pediatrician have decided to keep more than one feeding each night, schedule them for the first time your baby wakes after 10:00 p.m. and the first time they wake after 1:00 a.m. If your baby wakes substantially prior to the scheduled time (for example, baby wakes at 12:15 a.m., and their next scheduled feeding is at 1:00), do your checks and wait for them to fall back to sleep. Even if your baby is still awake at 1:00, wait until they fall back asleep, then feed them the next time they wake. Feeding baby after extended crying reinforces the waking, all but ensuring that they will continue crying for lengthy periods of time that night and on subsequent nights. Instead, aim to feed baby immediately upon waking, even if you decide to feed earlier than the scheduled time. Pick them up, nurse or bottle feed them, burp if needed, then put them back down. Falling asleep during a feeding is okay (once again, contrary to popular belief, it really isn't necessary to "wake them up" so they remember how to put themselves back to sleep on their own).

In the entirety of the Baby Sleep Trainer method, the most important set of directions have to do with what happens after 4:00 a.m., so whether you are keeping night feedings or not, it is extremely important that you follow these next directions as consistently as possible.

As we discussed in the Science of Sleep section, humans, babies especially, spend most of their early morning hours in light sleep. If you've ever woken up at 5:00 a.m. and realized you still had two hours before your alarm went off, you most likely turned over and waited for sleep to come again. That's because you know that, unless you went to bed at 9:00 the night before, your body isn't quite done sleeping, and that if you were to get up and start your day, you'd feel fatigued and slow. In most cases, adults can fall back into sleep after waking early in the morning and, if they're lucky, complete one or two more sleep cycles before having to get up. However, your infant or toddler doesn't know that when they wake up early, their body needs more sleep. If you have *any* interaction with your baby during those early morning hours, it is unlikely that they will fall back asleep. Also, they're likely to keep waking each morning around the same time with the expectation that you will return, so your timed checks will be ineffective and disruptive.

The best thing you can do, and the guideline you need to follow the *most closely*, is this: between 4:00 and 6:30 each morning, do not enter your child's room unless you suspect an emergency. It is extremely unlikely they will be awake for two and a half straight hours; instead, they will most likely eventually relax and go back to sleep. If your child is still asleep at 7:00, you'll want to get them up so they'll be ready for their first nap. If you have to consistently wake your child at 7:00, consider allowing them to wake up naturally, and make sure bedtime occurs about twelve hours *after* morning wake up. If your baby wakes at 8:00 a.m., schedule naps such that your child is ready for bed at 8:00 p.m.

If you are like the many families that need to get their child up earlier than 6:00 a.m., commit to staying out of the room from 4:00 a.m. until it's time to wake them up, and commit to a bedtime as close to twelve hours later as possible. A very important exception to the "no checks between 4:00 and 6:30 a.m." rule is if your child is keeping a night feeding and they do not wake up for their feeding until after 4:00. For example, if you have a single feeding scheduled for the first time your child wakes after 1:00 a.m., and they wake at 11:30 p.m., fall asleep at 12:00, and wake again at 4:30, that is technically the first time they are waking after 1:00 a.m., and they should be fed. Afterward, don't check on them (unless, of course, you suspect something is wrong) until it's time to start the day, preferably at or after 6:30.

It's possible, even likely, that by now you're feeling anxious, overwhelmed, reluctant, or incredulous that you can undertake sleep training. Please choose to trust in my extensive experience and in the hundreds of parents who have followed these guidelines to incredible success.

Twins

I thought hard about writing an entire chapter on twins, but the truth is it's actually relatively straightforward to sleep train twins. Essentially, parents have two choices: to train twins together in the same bedroom, or separately in different bedrooms. If possible, it's ideal to nap train twins in separate bedrooms, putting one baby in the master for naps while the other stays in the nursery. At night, babies have *so much* melatonin flowing through their bodies that they fall asleep quickly and stay asleep more deeply for longer periods of time than they're able to during the day, so unless you are adamant about using different rooms for overnight sleep training, it's usually fine to train twins together.

If you decide to train overnight in separate bedrooms, treat each baby as if they're going through sleep training independent of one another. Run two timers, two video monitors, and do individual checks for them all night long.

If you are keeping your twins in the same room, you can approach training in one of the following ways:

1. Select a "lead" baby, ideally whichever one tends to cry more than their sibling. You'll base your timed intervals and feedings (if keeping) on this baby. So, if the lead baby cries for ten straight minutes but

their sibling has only been crying intermittently, check on both babies at the same time. If the lead baby wakes at 1:30 a.m. to eat, wake and feed their sibling as well. Keep in mind that it is not *mandatory* to check on both babies at every check-in. If the easier-going twin seems to be nearly asleep while her sister has been crying for ten minutes, it's permissible to leave her be while doing a check on her crying sibling.

2.   Alternatively, you can attempt to train your twins independent of one another, even if they're in the same bedroom. This is easier when two adults (two parents or caregivers) are doing training together. In this scenario, each baby gets their own timer and is paired with one caretaker. If twin A is with Mom and B is with Dad, Dad runs the timer and checks on twin B, and only on twin B (since Mom is watching A). This works best when babies are young enough they don't notice when Mom or Dad walks into the room and *doesn't* check on them, then leaves.

Keep in mind that you can use instructions 1 above for night training babies in the same room, and instructions 2 for daytime nap training babies in two separate rooms (which is my preferred way to handle nighttime and daytime training for twins).

Twins usually do very well with sleep training because

not only are they accustomed to sharing space with their siblings, but because they seem to acclimate quickly to their sibling's cries. Time and again, I see twins sleeping deeply through their brother or sister wailing. Remain hyper-consistent, and make sure that above all else you focus on each child falling asleep completely on their own.

Common Issues That Arise During Nighttime Sleep Training

Here are the most commonly asked questions and the most frequently encountered issues families face during sleep training, and how to deal with each one.

1. My baby is flipping to their belly and can't flip back over.

   This is one of the questions that needs to be discussed with your pediatrician *before* you start training. I can almost guarantee you this issue will come up, and no one is better qualified to advise you than your doctor. Having said that, the American Academy of Pediatrics says that if your child is able to roll in both directions (back to stomach and stomach to back), it is acceptable to allow them to stay on their bellies if they roll there on their own. However, a vast majority of babies master the skill of rolling from back to belly months before they master flipping from belly to back, so it is imperative you follow your doctor's advice in this area.

2. How can I wean night feedings before starting night training?

First and foremost, never has the term "easier said than done" more aptly described a process than night weaning. Put simply, you will want to feed your child half an ounce by bottle, or one minute per nursing session, less for each established feeding every night until your child is down to one to two ounces or one to two minutes of nursing. This is easier said than done for two reasons. First, many children do not have established night feeds. They may graze repeatedly all night, or have irregular feeds, amounts, or nursing times. Second, babies usually don't notice that you are reducing their meals... until they do. Since you are trying to wean them down to one or no nighttime feedings, or however many your pediatrician says your baby needs, before starting training, this may mean that you will hit a point at which you have not reached that one-to-two ounce or minute reduction, but your baby is screaming because you have stopped them short of a full meal (that they may very well be relying on to fall asleep). If you find yourself in this position, soothe your child in any other way possible, then put them back down (asleep is fine), and continue until you're done weaning. If your pediatrician approves or advises you to do so, cutting feedings cold turkey can be easier on baby in the long run, as they will usually eat more the day following a night without feedings. Some, nay, *most* babies do not tolerate a slow weaning process and do better ripping off the Band-Aid, so to speak. Do not begin sleep training until your child is weaned down to your desired amount of feedings (unless you are going cold turkey, in which case you can stop them the first night of training).

3. How do I maintain my milk supply during training and beyond?

    I have never had a client inform me that they had to stop breastfeeding due to lack of supply associated with sleep training. This is because it is totally possible to maintain an abundant supply of milk while simultaneously teaching your child to fall asleep unassisted (which, if you recall, is all sleep training is). I would strongly advise that, until the month before you want to stop nursing, whether that's month six or twelve or any month at all, you commit to pumping every night before bed, sometime around 9:00 to 11:00 p.m. Even if you are maintaining a middle of the night feeding, pumping before bed is a good idea, and it's especially important once your baby is going twelve hours without nursing. In the following chapter, we will discuss nap training, but keep in mind that your younger baby will be eating every two-and-a-half to three-and-a-half hours throughout the day, and that your older infant should still be nursing at least four times each day. As long as you maintain a bedtime pumping session and make sure to nurse your child regularly during daytime hours, your milk supply should remain adequate. Whether sleep training or not, almost all women go through a period of time (usually around four to six months) during which they are all but certain their supply is diminishing. That's usually when the mother's body acclimates to her milk production and her breasts stop feeling full nonstop, like they do after birth. If you suspect at any moment your supply is diminishing or that your baby has stopped eating as much as they typically do, call your doctor and purchase an infant scale. I have seen countless friends spend weeks dealing with supply issues, going back and forth for weigh-ins, when weighing baby naked at home before and after each feeding will instantly confirm how much, exactly, their baby is consuming. Don't mess around with potential breast milk supply issues—often, identifying the problem early and addressing it immediately are all that's required for long term breastfeeding success.

4. My baby either falls asleep in an odd position, appears "stuck" while attempting to fall asleep (for

younger infants), or remains standing up (for older babies).

First and foremost, any issue arising out of a child's physical position should first be evaluated through a safety lens. If you think your child is in danger of being unable to breathe, *move them*! Generally, the possibility of obstructed breathing is what panics parents the most. If it is apparent your child can breathe, but you are still concerned about their position, consider the following: If your child falls asleep slumped over while seated, or in any other seemingly unsafe position, consider moving them if you think they aren't able to breathe easily. Make sure you can see them breathing on the monitor or watch from inside their bedroom, and try to give them several minutes to fall into deeper sleep before repositioning them. If your child is still awake but has gotten stuck in a corner, reposition them only if you think they are in danger of getting hurt or not being able to breathe. You want to let your baby figure out how to move around and use all the space in their crib to be comfortable, so it's not necessary to keep them in a single spot. Doing a 180 or scooting all over is normal. If your child is stuck in a standing position, help them lie down without starting a game in which you lie them down and they stand up again. Again, evaluate this first from a perspective of safety.

Leaving baby to stand shouldn't be harmful, and they do eventually need to learn to sit down on their own. Check with the pediatrician, and if s/he approves, feel free to allow your baby to stand as long as they like, and eventually they will realize how to get down and go to sleep on their own.

5. I want my baby to be on an 8:00 a.m. to 8:00 p.m. (or later) schedule.

The reason I advise my clients to have a bedtime as close to 7:00 p.m. as possible is not because earlier bedtimes are healthier for baby (although they absolutely are), but because regardless of when you put your baby down, in the overwhelming majority of cases, they will wake sometime around 7:00 a.m., if not earlier, to start their day. Even in cases where baby is still getting a night feed, they often can't drowse through that early morning light stage sleep.

Your baby needs about eleven to twelve hours of nighttime sleep, so if they are consistently starting their day between 6:30 and 7:00 a.m., they need a bedtime about twelve hours before then. In cases where your child is waking earlier than 6:30, but you are waiting to start your day until then, you should count the start of their day as the moment they get up and are exposed to direct sunlight and fed for the first time. If you force your child to stay awake until a later bedtime and they still wake early in the morning, you are robbing them of nighttime sleep. If, in an effort to achieve a later bedtime, you allow your child to nap later into the afternoon (past about 4:00), you are more likely to disrupt their overall circadian rhythm and cause more nighttime wake ups. It would be like if you took an hour-long nap at 7:00 and tried to go to bed at 10:00—that evening nap would disrupt your body's wake/sleep cycle as much as drinking a big cup of coffee late in the day.

The bottom line is that children can vary widely in their habits and tendencies, so if your child naturally wakes after 7:00, feel free to honor their later sleep patterns. But just remember you're not likely to get a later wake up time just by putting them to bed later the night before.

6. I need to start my baby's day earlier than 6:30.

Many families need to start their day earlier than 6:30 for one reason or another. My advice is to keep your baby in their crib until as close to 6:30 as possible, and then try very hard to get them down each night about twelve hours after they wake up for the day. Also, especially for babies six months and older, even with a wake time earlier than 6:30, don't start their first morning nap earlier than 8:30 or 9:00 unless they are going to bed before 6:30 p.m. An earlier first nap can cause your baby to have a very difficult time making it to 6:00 or 6:30 p.m., as it leads to a shifting up of all naps, leaving a long gap between the end of the last nap of the day and bedtime.

7. My baby wakes up too early in the morning.

Early morning waking and short naps are the two most common problems to persist even after weeks of training. Again, because of light stage sleep after about 4:00 a.m., some babies struggle with sleeping in. Make sure during the first month of sleep training in particular that you remain consistent about not doing checks (except in case of emergency) between 4:00 and 6:30. Sometimes early morning waking just takes a while to resolve itself.

If you are still struggling, attempt to look at your child's overall sleep patterns. As we will discuss in the following chapter, evaluate if your child is ready to reduce the number of naps they are taking each day; a child who is seven months old, taking three naps, and waking at 5:15 a.m. will probably start sleeping in later if you reduce their naps to two per day. If you feel you are at the correct number of naps, evaluate overall daily nap duration. Consider shaving ten to fifteen minutes off total daytime sleep every three to five days until you've reduced daytime sleep by thirty to sixty minutes. Finally, try moving bedtime ten to fifteen minutes later every few nights until it's thirty to forty-five minutes later than it was originally (try this before or after reducing the number of naps and total duration of daytime sleep, not at the same time). Finally, for babies taking just one nap, make sure that it isn't ending later than about 3:30 p.m.

8. I've heard that sometimes babies vomit during sleep training.

This is something that happens during other forms of sleep training, but almost never when using the Baby Sleep Trainer method. For some babies, crying easily turns into vomiting; if that sounds familiar, ask your pediatrician what you should do if your baby throws up while going through the process.

Vomiting also sometimes occurs after interaction with caregivers that is too frequent or hands-on during check-ins. The key is to make sure not to panic baby, which usually happens if you're overly interactive during training, without ultimately helping baby fall asleep, making them more upset.

I have had a number of clients who, regardless of what they do, have children who throw up during sleep training. Their doctors usually advise them to clean their babies completely, clean the surrounding area, and resume training. If your child vomits easily and your pediatrician says to continue with training, you generally should not feed baby again to "replace" whatever your baby threw up, as this can cause them to vomit again. As with everything, talk to your doctor and follow their advice.

9. What should I do about soiled diapers during the 4:00 to 6:30 a.m. no-check-in period?

If you know at any time of the day or night that your baby has soiled their diaper, change them. If you find that your child has been pooping between 4:00 a.m. and whenever it's time for them to start the day, evaluate what you are feeding them and when. Often, playing around with the timing of dinner, or the foods baby is eating, can change your baby's pooping schedule. Generally, babies only poop early in the morning for a short while before starting to go again at different times of day. If you suspect they have pooped after 4:00 a.m., quietly go in and do a quick sniff check—if necessary, change baby and put them back down. If you keep going in and *not* finding a soiled diaper, scale back your checks.

10. What should I do if we're traveling in the middle of training, or after we finish training?

Similar rules apply to traveling as when you are dealing with illness. Your primary focus should be ensuring that you are not helping your child fall asleep. Simple things like putting your baby down awake and then stepping out of the hotel room into the hallway for a few minutes while they fall asleep is a good idea, as is lining the *outside* perimeter of your infant's Pack n' Play-style porta-crib with pillows so they can't see you while sharing a room (this only works, of course, if your baby isn't able to sit or stand up). Make sure to pack a white noise machine, painter's tape, and tinfoil so you can cover up any windows that let in light.

Despite your best efforts, you may find yourself having to calm a screaming baby before they wake up a beach house full of your closest relatives, and in extenuating circumstances you may have no other choice than to help them fall asleep. In this case, get back to allowing your child to fall asleep independently as soon as possible. Know that the first forty-eight hours of baby falling asleep on their own again will be much like the first two days of sleep training, so remain consistent and baby should get back on track quickly. If you are on an airplane or in a car, it is acceptable to help your child fall asleep however you can, so don't worry about trying to keep them on schedule while in various modes of transportation. Finally, try to honor your child's need to sleep as much as possible, especially the first nap of each day, by letting them take as many naps as possible in the hotel room or bedroom you're staying in. It's understandable to be a bit "off" during trips; just make sure you come back home ready for consistency in letting your child get to sleep on their own. If necessary, restart training at bedtime as outlined in this book, and you will be back on track in a few days.

11. Can I dreamfeed instead of a middle-of-the-night feed?

As discussed in the Newborn Sleep section, dreamfeeds are great for babies who are still swaddled and younger than sixteen weeks, but they aren't useful for babies past that stage and age. If only our babies were like little cars, with tanks we could fill up at any time to fuel them through the night. Alas, attempting to feed a sleeping baby at 10:00 p.m. will not prevent hunger from waking them at 2:00 a.m., and worse, dreamfeeding a baby past the newborn stage is generally disruptive to nighttime sleep. Fracturing sleep in that manner, even if it doesn't rouse baby all the way, can cause disrupted sleep for the rest of the night and prompt your baby to start waking up each night around the time of their dreamfeed. If your baby needs to eat overnight, feed them when they wake up and are hungry, preferably the first time they wake after 1:00 a.m.

12. Are verbal checks through the monitor okay?

If you are going to check on your child, do so in person. Talking through the monitor can alarm children of all ages, and can become one more thing they're reliant on or expecting in order to go to sleep.

13. How do I know if it's an emergency?

If you think *anything* might be an emergency, check on your child immediately and address the issue. As long as you don't take the next step of helping them falling asleep, feel free to go in at any time. Instead of outlining what's an emergency and what isn't, you should rely on your own instincts and observations. Just remember, do *not* help your child fall asleep after you've addressed whatever is going on.

Troubleshooting After Sleep Training

The last and perhaps most important question that I get is: How do I deal with things like illness, teething, separation anxiety, or sleep regressions during training, or after training is finished? Every time I finish a consultation with a client, I share a key piece of information on how to make sure they never, ever have to sleep train again.

Here it is: No matter what is causing a nighttime waking, do *not* help your child fall back to sleep. If your child wakes up because they are ill, get them up, treat them however your pediatrician recommends, stay physically present, and comfort them until they show signs of tiredness (try sitting in a room with very low to no lighting), and put them back down—awake. Resume checks if needed, but do not help them fall asleep. Once they are asleep, I encourage you to go back and room share, sleeping on the floor, an air mattress, or a nearby bed. You want to be with them in case they wake up and need you, but not as they fall asleep; that they must do on their own. If you do not follow this one piece of advice and you stay with them as they fall asleep or help them in any other way, they *will* regress with their sleep training, and you will have to do it all over again. This advice applies to naps as well, so make sure that you are not "helping" your child get rest during illness by holding or otherwise helping them fall asleep. If they are tired and need to sleep, they will be able to do so on their own in their crib.

I often get emails from clients saying something like, "Tommy got sick three weeks ago and wouldn't fall asleep until XYZ (feeding, rocking, holding, etc.), and now he's up a few times each night and won't fall asleep for naps and bedtime until I do XYZ." There should be no "until." Simply operate under the assumption that you're physically unable to help your child fall asleep. You can spend hours with them in the middle of the night watching shows or reading books or holding them or talking to them until they feel better, and you should watch closely as they are falling asleep to make sure they are safe, but do not help them fall asleep, unless your pediatrician specifically advises otherwise.

This guideline extends to every other sleep disruption, from cognitive leaps to the oft cited but not scientifically-supported "sleep regressions" occurring at certain ages. No matter what has woken your child up, go to them, address the issue if possible, and put them down awake. Keep an eye out during teething and other disturbances with causes that are harder to identify. If you start treating your child for teething symptoms, and after a few days you notice that their nighttime wakings have increased, it may be that they're not actually teething, or not still teething, but are still waking for you to come visit. As soon as you notice increased night wakings with no clear cause, you are on the path to unraveling all of your hard work. Go back to the plan, resume check-ins if needed, and start to scale back your presence at night.

Recap

- Sleep training should begin at bedtime, never at naptime or in the middle of the night.

- Bedtime should ideally be between 6:30 and 7:30 p.m., unless extenuating circumstances dictate otherwise.

- Put your child down wholly awake after a brief soothing period, and do checks at predetermined intervals, preferably as close to ten minutes (or longer) as possible.

- Restart your timer when baby takes any pauses whatsoever in crying longer than three to five seconds, and commit to only checking if baby has been crying for the full length of the interval.

- Don't do more than four or five checks in a row, since at that point it's likely your child will stay awake as long as you continue to check on them. Stop your checks, allow them to fall asleep on their own, and resume checks (or do a scheduled feeding) the next time they wake, as long as it's before 4:00 a.m.

- Finally, and most importantly, don't do any checks from 4:00 to 6:30 a.m., except in case of emergency, and with exceptions noted in this chapter. Ideally, your child will be out of their crib sometime between 6:30 and 7:00 a.m. each day.

Nighttime Sleep Training Cheat Sheet

Pick baby's bedtime (page X)

Understand the 1-10 wakefulness scale & watch closely (page X)

Establish your short, simple bedtime and final feeding routine (page X)

Put baby to bed utilizing the five-minute soothing technique (page X)

Review how to handle check-ins and pauses (page X)

Review what to do when baby wakes up again before 4:00 am (page X)

Abide by the no check-in rule between 4:00 am - 6:30 am, with outlined exceptions (page X)

Review nighttime feedings procedure (page X)

Would you like to work with me on

a more
personal level?

I offer one-on-one consultations
and an in-depth online training
series to fit any budget.

To learn more check out
www.babysleeptrainer.com

Nap Training

Simultaneous Nap and Nighttime Training

IT HAS ALWAYS been a mystery to me why more sleep experts don't *insist* on the importance of nighttime and nap training at the same time. Not a week goes by that I don't receive a phone call from a parent, often in tears, about how sleep training is simply "not working," and upon asking a few questions I find out that a book, or even another consultant, has led them to believe it's normal or more humane to "take care of night sleep first, then deal with naps." Nothing could be further from the truth.

Recently, I had a mother tell me that she had been implementing extinction-style (no checks whatsoever for twelve hours) sleep training for over two months with her one-year-old son. He was waking up each night from 3:00 to 4:30 a.m., crying, falling asleep for twenty minutes, then waking up again and staying awake until morning. Upon further questioning, I discovered that she was putting him down at 9:00 each morning for a nap in his crib, which he was not falling asleep for—and that later in the day he would take a two-hour nap in the stroller with the nanny. This mother was at a complete loss as to why her son couldn't sleep through the night. I quickly identified that because he was getting "help" to fall asleep for his nap, he couldn't understand why he wasn't getting help to fall asleep in the middle of the night as well. I told her that his nighttime problems wouldn't cease until he was putting himself to sleep 100 percent of the time.

One of the only situations in which I will refuse to take on a client is when they are unwilling to nap and nighttime sleep train at the same time. Training a child to sleep at night before attempting to tackle naps is often the least humane path a parent can take. As we've discussed, nighttime sleep training tends to be relatively easy, because the body is flooded with melatonin around bedtime, making it easy and pleasant for kids to give into sleep. But it becomes harder and harder for children to fall back asleep as night turns into morning. If a child is not skilled at falling back asleep during the lighter stages of their sleep cycle, they will struggle to sleep through the night. If children are only trained at nighttime, they may succeed in temporarily sleeping a solid twelve hours at night, but will often vociferously fight sleep during the day. Their parents don't realize that their child now has so much stamina and energy from sleeping through the night that they are able to fight naps almost completely—and the older a child is when starting nap training, the longer they will likely fight it. When parents only want to teach their baby to sleep through the night, but also want to continue to nap them on the go, or however they currently sleep during the day, they will almost always find that it is only a matter of time before their child begins to struggle to fall back asleep in between sleep cycles at night. Sometimes the regression in nighttime sleep is spontaneous, but usually it is due to travel or illness, at which time their child is no longer willing to fall asleep without assistance, and then any progress they've made at night vanishes. I implore you not to put your child through any type of sleep training unless you are able and willing to nap and nighttime train at the same time.

When a child is in daycare, it can be very difficult (though not impossible) to do both nighttime and daytime training simultaneously. For parents whose children are in full time daycare, I suggest starting nighttime training on a Friday night and staying home for the entire weekend to focus on naps. If possible, take Friday and/or Monday off in order to tackle nap training for three or four days straight—one to two weeks at home to focus on sleep training would be even better! Once a baby returns to daycare, parents should ask daycare providers to use white noise and darkness to encourage them to transfer the skills they learned at home into the daycare environment. Small, at-home-style daycare centers are often more willing to accommodate parents' requests, and are sometimes even able to put children to nap in a separate bedroom, away from the hum and buzz of the rest of the daycare's activities. Children often struggle to nap at larger, more corporate daycares, but parents should still focus for several days on intense nap and nighttime training, and see how their child sleeps once they return. Hands down, the one thing parents must insist on with their daycare providers is that once baby or toddler returns with the skill of being able to fall asleep unassisted, caretakers should *never* revert to helping the child fall asleep. If caretakers are insistent on helping your child fall asleep for any reason, consider whether you want to undertake the sleep training process at all. As we've discussed, it is imperative that children be able to put themselves to sleep completely at all times if you want them to keep sleeping through the night.

For anyone who is currently debating whether to hire a nanny or put baby in daycare, I would encourage you to select the first option if it's within your means. While daycare has many wonderful benefits, including increased socialization for baby and more reliability for parents— daycares don't call in sick, quit, or stop showing up from one day to the next—it is usually less optimal when it comes to sleep. (Around fourteen to eighteen months, when children go down to one nap per day, daycare is a wonderful choice. The "mass mentality" of their peers falling asleep around them seems to encourage even the most active child to calm down and go to sleep.) I have had many families leave or switch daycares when they realize that the center their child attends is the root of their sleep problems. But take comfort in the fact that most daycares, especially at-home daycares, are more than willing to accommodate parents in whatever way they can, so asking for minor changes can go a long way towards helping your child maintain the environment they need in order to nap well during the day—and keep everyone happy at home.

How Many Naps Does My Child Need?

Before you commit to the task of nap training your child, evaluate first how many naps they need each day. For the most part, the number of naps a child needs correlates to their age, but the phrase "every child is different" applies here. The method outlined in this chapter is applicable to children of all ages *if they are still sleeping in a crib.* If your child is sleeping in a regular bed, move on to the Sleep Training Children in Beds section.

Four to seven months

Generally speaking, a child four to seven months old should be napping three times each day. If they are on a roughly 7:00 a.m. to 7:00 p.m. schedule, naps should occur around 8:30 a.m., 11:30 a.m., and 3:00 p.m. each day, with feedings after waking in the morning and after each nap, with the last feed taking place half an hour before bedtime. Many children in this age range are also feeding at least once overnight, so it shouldn't be necessary to feed them more frequently than at these times. (I'll discuss feedings in more detail at the end of this chapter.)

Sample schedule for a three-nap baby:

6:30-7:00 a.m.: wake, milk feeding

8:30: nap

Wake, milk feeding

11:30: nap

Wake, milk feeding

3:00 p.m.: nap

Wake, milk feeding

6:30: final milk feeding, bedtime preparations

7:00: bedtime

1:00 a.m.: night feeding

Note that there are no times listed for when baby should wake from each nap. I'll discuss this in further detail later in the chapter, but suffice it to say that *how long a baby sleeps should not determine when their next nap starts*. Using the length of time a baby has been awake (i.e., "wake times") to calculate when they should next nap will cause chaos in both baby's and parent's life. If a baby takes a nap of any length, they should be put to sleep as close as possible to their next scheduled naptime.

Seven to fourteen months

Children in this age range typically need only two naps each day, around 9:00 a.m. and 1:30 p.m., if on a 7-to-7 schedule. It's imperative that the second nap start around 1:30 p.m. so that the gap between the end of nap two and bedtime is as short as possible. Again, if still nursing or bottle feeding, aim for feedings to occur after morning wake up, after each of the two naps, and half an hour before bedtime. If your child is not yet eating solids consistently, consider adding in another milk feeding around noon. If your child *is* eating solids, aim to feed them breakfast about an hour after morning wake up, lunch around noon, dinner about two hours after waking from their second nap (which should be about two hours before bedtime). Most babies should not need a night feed unless the child's pediatrician has indicated they still do.

Sample schedule for a two-nap baby:

6:30-7:00 a.m.: wake, milk feeding

8:00: breakfast solids

9:00: nap

Wake, milk feeding

12:00 p.m.: milk feeding or lunch solids (it is especially easy for baby to become drowsy during this milk feeding due to its proximity to naptime, so work hard to keep your child fully awake)

1:30: nap

Wake, milk feeding

5:00: dinner solids

6:30: final milk feeding, bedtime preparations

7:00: bedtime

Fourteen months and beyond

Toddlers around fourteen to eighteen months typically only need one nap each day, starting sometime between 11:30 a.m. and 1:00 p.m., and lasting one-and-a-half to three hours, depending on the child. A child taking one nap each day is usually getting all or most of their calories from solid food and liquids (milk, etc.) via sippy cup. Feeding times can be adjusted as needed. Unless your pediatrician recommends otherwise, it's likely no longer necessary to provide a milk feeding half an hour before bed.

Now that we've established the general rules of thumb, how can you know how many naps your child needs? Sleep training books make it seem easy to decide, but it can be difficult to decide how many naps are optimal for your child.

For babies months four through six, start with the assumption that they need three naps. If they are especially strong willed and are only falling asleep twice during the day, even after ten to fourteen days of nap training, consider moving down to two naps. While your child may benefit from three naps, if they won't allow themselves to fall asleep that many times each day, it will behoove them to learn to consolidate all of their daytime sleep into just two. Conversely, perhaps you have a four-and-a-half month old who consistently naps two hours each morning, making it difficult to squeeze in three naps each day. Later on in this chapter, we will discuss why it's important to end naps around 4:00 each afternoon, but if naps are ending then, it may be impossible to fit in a third. Rest assured that your infant can get all of their necessary sleep each day, even if they're just taking two naps.

If your child is seven to fourteen months old, assume they need two naps each day. In almost every case, that holds true through *at least* their first birthday. Almost all children go through a phase around ten or eleven months, sometimes lasting up to a month, during which they refuse one of their naps each day. Naturally, parents begin to think that this fighting of a nap (usually nap two) is an indication that their child only needs one nap each day. This typical regression tends to pass within one or two weeks, so parents shouldn't change anything about their daily patterns. When your child is approaching the age at which it is appropriate to switch them to one nap, you will know because their behavior meets one of the following criteria:

1. Your child is over fourteen months of age and has consistently fought one of their two naps each day for two weeks straight or longer.

2. Your child naps easily twice each day, but struggles

to fall asleep before 9:00 or 10:00 each night, or begins to wake up in the middle of the night.

A note on scheduling: For most babies and families, a roughly 7:00 a.m. to 7:00 p.m. schedule seems to work best. If a 7-to-7 schedule can work for your family, I encourage you to make an effort to follow the nap times outlined below. For a variety of reasons, many families are unable to follow a 7-to-7 schedule, or may simply feel their child would thrive with naps and bedtime at different times than I've outlined in this chapter. Either way, don't be discouraged—do what you feel works best for your family and baby, implementing these nap training strategies as consistently as possible.

Nap training can be very challenging. It requires a substantial amount of commitment and stamina from parents, and it will be *extremely* tempting to deviate from the methods described below. Generally speaking, parents should count on nap training taking one to two weeks. In order for nap training to be successful, parents must start the morning after the first night of sleep training. Some babies take to nap training immediately; some need a few weeks. In most cases, it takes at least a week for it to really stick. In the first few days, some babies can appear to sleep well, only to struggle with naps on day three or four. This is likely because during the first days of training, they were making up for lost sleep, and the real training has only started now.

Do _not_ begin the sleep training process until you can dedicate a full forty-eight to ninety-six hours— the longer the better—to staying physically home with your baby. This means no car seats, strollers, or carriers, and no walks to get the mail or taking the dog around the block or trips to the grocery store. If you take your baby out during the first few days of nap training, they will almost certainly fall asleep, causing a major regression in your progress and equaling more tears for baby.

It is impossible to overemphasize that the number one most important guideline to follow during nap training is _do not help your child fall asleep._ If your baby is with you, they must be fully awake (between a one and a three on the one-to-ten wakefulness scale). Even and especially while they are having feedings, you need to ensure that they stay fully awake. If you notice your baby starting to become drowsy, stop the feeding and wake them fully, then feed them again. If you allow or assist your child to fall asleep, you will sabotage the program and make things very difficult on your baby. Don't give them a "break" and "help" them nap in your arms or stroller at the end of a day of poor naps—your number one job for several weeks is to be hyper-vigilant and ensure that under no circumstances are you purposefully allowing your baby to fall asleep anywhere other than on their own in their crib.

Keep in mind that the first forty-eight hours are often the most challenging. You are changing many things for your baby all at once. Parents implore me all the time for a more gradual approach, but the truth is the more reluctantly a parent approaches nap training, the more likely they are to draw the process out for their baby, meaning more tears and lack of sleep. Strive to commit to the first forty-eight hours and each day thereafter, and your child will eventually be successful in getting as much sleep as their bodies need. It may be the case that baby plateaus for up to ten days, seemingly making no progress in the lengths of their naps, before finally "getting it" and taking longer naps. You should be prepared to commit to this training method for about two weeks in order for your baby to be fully successful.

Once you have determined how many naps your baby needs, you can focus on the relevant section below, but I would recommend reading all three; much of the information is relevant no matter how many naps your child is taking.

Three naps

Regardless of what time your child woke up in the morning, you will be getting them out of their crib between 6:30 and 7:00. (If your schedule dictates they wake up earlier, bedtime should be roughly twelve hours after they get out of their crib in the morning, so adjust the following times accordingly.) Baby's first nap should occur no earlier than 8:30, even if before training they are accustomed to napping earlier.

Upon waking, feed your baby immediately, then go about your normal morning activities. At first, most babies will begin to get drowsy before 8:30, but do your best to keep them engaged and happy until as close to then as possible. Direct exposure to sunlight or playing in an infant bath with water can help babies get past a fussy stage. Even though it may seem counterintuitive to keep your baby up when they want to sleep, helping their brains and bodies become accustomed to staying awake until a certain time each morning will quickly help them develop a consistent nap pattern. There's a lot of information out there about avoiding overtiredness, but the truth is that this is something that often plagues newborns but doesn't really affect older infants. As we discussed in the Science of Sleep chapter, the reason babies wake from a nap after thirty minutes has to do with an inability to link sleep cycles or consolidate daytime sleep, or both—not because they're "too tired" to nap.

Commit to feeding your baby only upon waking, and focus on completing a full feed. This should be easy if your child has only had one or no feedings the previous night. Once they are done with their first feeding of the day, do not feed them again until they get up from their first nap attempt.

At 8:30 a.m., walk into your baby's room, close the curtains, turn on the white noise, and repeat the five minute soothing routine you did at bedtime the night before. To review: Set a five-minute timer—a cell phone placed in your back pocket is perfect. Remember, from the moment your baby was taken out of their crib in the morning until the moment you walk into their room, they should have been kept fully awake, between a one and a three on the wakefulness scale. Hold your baby, *avoiding any and all movements you think will make them sleepy or drowsy*, and aim to get them from a one to a five on the wakefulness scale. A five would be your baby yawning, rubbing their eyes, or rubbing their face into your shoulder. This can be achieved by standing very still, walking baby slowly around the room, or very gently rocking them. Your goal is to help your baby be calm and awake when they go in the crib, *not* sleepy or drowsy. Because so many parents have heard that they should put baby down "drowsy but awake," they don't realize that that's the most difficult way for your child to fall asleep. If they are nearly asleep but not all the way out, they will wake up instantly upon being put down and, because their body had already starting going into a sleep cycle, it will be several minutes before they are ready to fall asleep again. Instead, make sure to place your child in their crib on their back the moment you see them show a tired sign, or once you feel the timer go off in your pocket. Give them a kiss and walk out of the room. This will be a radical change if you are accustomed to putting them down asleep, but your child will have had the previous night to practice. Also, the soothing process before naptime should be identical to the soothing process before bedtime. If your child cries and protests loudly the whole five minutes you're with them, consider reducing the timer to one or two minutes, but try the soothing technique for the full five minutes for a few days first.

Once baby is down, they will have one hour to attempt to fall asleep. Within that hour, there are only three possibilities.

1. Baby falls asleep, and sleeps for less than forty-five minutes. If this occurs, instead of running right in when you hear them rouse, instead give them ten to fifteen minutes to attempt to fall back to sleep (after all, the only reason they woke up was because they completed one sleep cycle and were having trouble entering the next one). If baby falls back to sleep, get them up the next time they wake, and make sure they do not sleep for more than 120 minutes during the entire nap. Remember, don't count time in the crib, count actual time asleep. If baby does *not* fall back asleep, get them up after ten to fifteen minutes and immediately feed them, making *certain* they do not fall asleep or become drowsy. Regardless of how short the nap was, they should be kept awake until their next scheduled naptime (review the previous section to continue with the sample schedule).

2. Baby falls asleep and sleeps past the forty-five-minute mark. This means your baby has completed one full sleep cycle and has successfully linked to the next! Anytime baby wakes up between minute forty-six and minute 120, get them up, feed them, and move on

with the day. Do not allow your baby to sleep longer than two hours during a single nap and always make sure there is at least a ninety-to-105-minute gap from the end of their nap to the start of the next one. In rare instances, babies sleep so long during their first nap that they are unable to fit in a third nap that ends by 4:00 p.m. If this happens, consider doing just two naps that day, with the second starting around 1:30 or 2:00, keeping bedtime at the same time or moving it earlier by thirty minutes.

3. Baby refuses sleep for the full hour. In this scenario, you should get baby up and feed them immediately (since it's been about three hours since their last feeding), while making 100 percent certain they do *not fall asleep* while eating. Thirty minutes later, put them down for another one-hour nap attempt. For example, if baby went down at 8:30 a.m. and did not fall asleep for the full hour, they should be gotten up at 9:30, fed, kept awake until 10:00, and then put back down for another one-hour nap attempt, during which they will either take a short nap of less than forty-five minutes, a long nap of more than forty-five minutes, or no nap at all. Depending on which scenario occurs, follow the guidelines above.

As you go through the first few days of training, you'll want to set aside the importance of a schedule and instead focus on the following guidelines:

- Start your baby's day between 6:30 and 7:00 a.m.

- Aim for nap one to start as close to 8:30 a.m. as possible.

- Do not allow baby to nap past 4:00 p.m.

- If baby gets *any* amount of sleep for a nap, don't put them down again until the next scheduled naptime, or as close as possible.

- Checks similar to those during night training are permissible, but know that for many babies, interaction during naptime hinders their efforts to fall asleep, so proceed cautiously avoid doing checks during naps if at all possible.

A note on feedings: If you aim to feed your baby after they wake up from each nap attempt, they will be eating every two-and-a-half to three-and-a-half hours throughout the day. Thus, I would strongly caution against feeding them *again* before a nap. In most cases, when a parent thinks a baby is hungry close to naptime, the baby is in fact simply tired, which is why they so easily fall asleep when offered milk. You want to break the connection between eating and sleeping. Having said that, you are the only one who is uniquely capable of deciding whether or not your child needs a feed. If you need to feed your baby anytime other than right after a nap, make certain they stay completely awake during the entire feeding.

As I've emphasized repeatedly in this chapter and in

other parts of the book, it is very important that your child be awake when they are with you and only fall asleep when they are on their own in their crib. However, in the first few days of training and especially with younger infants, sometimes it will feel *impossible* to keep your baby awake. They may even fall asleep while playing under a baby gym! If your baby falls asleep independently outside of their crib, allow them to remain asleep and do not move them. Perhaps turn off the lights in the room and put a white noise machine near where they are sleeping. Observe them and allow them to sleep as long as they want while observing the guidelines above. Once they wake on their own, move on with the rest of the day, making sure their final nap does not end past 4:00 p.m.

Two naps

There are many similarities in nap training all children, so make sure to read the outline for three nap babies *before* you continue with the method for your two-nap child. Thankfully, the fewer naps a baby takes, the more straightforward nap training tends to be. Older infants generally handle less daytime sleep (which is common in the first days and weeks of nap training) better than younger babies.

Get your baby out of their crib between 6:30 and 7:00 a.m. and give them a feeding right away. If they are eating solids, offer them breakfast about an hour after they wake. Around 9:00 (or anytime prior to 10:00), enter their room and put them down with the five-minute soothing technique. Your baby will also get one hour to attempt to fall asleep, but we will not focus on the length of their nap.

1. If your baby falls asleep at any point and sleeps for any amount of time, get them up as soon as they wake up and offer them a milk feeding. Keep them awake until as close as possible to their next scheduled nap-time (1:30 p.m. or later). Alternatively, if you deem a nap to be too short, you can wait about ten to twenty minutes to give baby a chance to fall back to sleep before getting them up. If they do fall back asleep, get them up the next time they wake, and do not allow them to sleep for more than 120 total minutes.

2. If your baby does not fall asleep during the hour, get them up and give them a milk feeding (keeping them *totally* awake), then put them down thirty minutes later for another one-hour attempt.

Assuming that they are taking naps around 9:00 or 10:00, and again around 1:30 or 2:30, you may get into a tricky situation if your baby does not nap on their first attempt, and then falls asleep during their second. If they take a nap around midday and it lasts for seventy-five or more minutes, decide whether it makes sense to offer them another nap. If you think they can fall asleep again and be awake no later than 4:00, give baby a one-hour nap attempt no later than 3:00. But, if your baby falls asleep for the first time around noon and sleeps until about 2:00, they likely will not be able or willing to fall asleep again before having to be up by 4:00. In this case, you can do an early bedtime, as early as 6:00 p.m., and be consistent the next morning by starting baby's days no earlier than 6:30 in the morning.

The same guidelines apply as for three nap babies: stay home for the first two to four days, no napping past 4:00, no single nap longer than two hours, and check-ins are fine as long as they don't appear to make baby more frustrated and upset.

One nap

Nap training a baby who only needs one nap a day is a double-edged sword. On the one hand, toddlers tend to tolerate missing a nap relatively well, but on the other, they can elect to nap strike for weeks, fighting naps each day and not allowing themselves to nap for many days in a row. Thankfully, most toddlers take to nap training within the first ten days, just like most other babies. Again, it will be helpful to read through the nap training method for babies on three and two naps, as both those scenarios include relevant details to single-nap babies.

Milk is likely no longer your toddler's primary form of nutrition, so making sure your baby is getting enough calories is a bit easier. After getting your child up for the day between 6:30 and 7:00 a.m., feed them breakfast, and perhaps a snack a few hours later.

Starting between 11:00 and 11:30 a.m., put your child down for an attempt following the same five minute calming technique described above, again giving them one hour (or up to ninety minutes if you feel your child would benefit from having more time to attempt to fall asleep) to try to fall asleep on their own. At this age, check-ins are almost always detrimental, so it may be better if you allow your child to be on their own throughout their attempt. If your child falls asleep for any length of time, get them up as soon as they wake, and keep them up until bedtime. Feel free to move bedtime earlier by up to one hour if needed to accommodate a short or early nap.

If your toddler does not fall asleep, offer them up to two more attempts. A sample training schedule might look like:

11:00 a.m.-12:00 p.m.: nap attempt one

12:30-1:30: nap attempt two

2:00-3:00: nap attempt three

Early bedtime if no successful naps.

If they refuse to nap all day, be especially careful that they not fall asleep anywhere before bedtime. Babies who only nap once a day should be allowed to sleep up to three hours, but naptime should end not later than 3:30.

How to transition to fewer naps

Once sleep training is complete, there will come a time when you need to transition to fewer naps. Anytime you make that shift, your child may be tired throughout the process. That's normal, so if you're certain your child is ready, per the guidelines below, don't let their tiredness keep you from reducing to the appropriate number of naps.

Three to two

The three-to-two transition can be tricky to navigate. Your child will be ready to go down to two naps when they are:

1. Not falling asleep for all three naps (because they are not tired enough for nap three);

2. Falling asleep for all three naps but struggling to fall asleep at bedtime or waking at night or early in the morning, unable to go back to sleep; or

3. Able to fall asleep three times each day, but the last nap is so late that it goes past 4:00 p.m.

Once you decide that it's time to transition to two naps, simply put your child down at 9:00 a.m. and 1:30 p.m., and move bedtime earlier if you need to. This transition usually only takes seven to ten days, so remain consistent and do not go back and forth between three and two naps.

Two to one

When it comes time to transition your toddler to just one nap each day, know that it will be about thirty days before they consolidate all of their daytime sleep into one nap. During this month long period, do not add in a second nap just because your child's daily nap was only forty-five minutes. Keep them awake until bedtime, perhaps putting them down thirty minutes earlier than normal, but *do not* go back and forth between one and two naps.

At this age, shifting nap schedules is fairly straightforward. You can always go cold turkey and keep your child awake until about 11:00 a.m., put them down for a nap, and then keep them awake until bedtime. I prefer to adjust children slowly, moving their first nap of the day about fifteen minutes later every two to three days, while continuing to put them down for about thirty minutes around 2:00 p.m. every day (with the assumption being they will not sleep, just simply "rest" in their crib in their room with the lights off and white noise on). Once the first nap starts at 11:00, stop putting your child down in the afternoon, but continue to move the 11:00 nap gradually later until it starts at what you deem to be an appropriate time for your child (around 12:00 to 1:00 p.m. for most children).

Still thinking you may

WANT SOME
EXTRA HELP?

Check out my online training
series or one-on-one
consultation packages.

www.babysleeptrainer.com

SLEEP TRAINING CHILDREN IN BEDS

WHEN CLIENTS CALL asking for help training their kiddos who are no longer in cribs, I inform them that training older toddlers is more "dramatic (for the child) and traumatic (for the parents)" than working with babies, but with the added benefit of the entire process usually working much more quickly. If you haven't read my pleas in earlier chapters, let me reiterate how important it is to keep your children in cribs as long as possible. A child can safely stay in their crib through the age of four provided they are not attempting to climb out, and you should never move them from their crib before then unless there are safety reasons to do so. If you have a child who must be sleep trained in a bed instead of a crib, you will find clear directions below for how to help them learn to sleep through the night and take healthy naps. As always, these suggestions should be okay'd by your pediatrician before starting the training program.

Nighttime Sleep Training

The age that children may be sleep trained in a bed varies widely, from as young as seventeen months (usually about when some kiddos crawl out of the cribs) to three-and-a-half years old. While older children can be sleep trained, these methods are meant for those three-and-a-half and younger. Unfortunately, the most challenging age for sleep training is between seventeen months and two-and-a-half years, since younger toddlers are not able to understand many of the techniques that are used to compel older toddlers to choose to stay in their rooms and go to sleep. If you need to train a child in that range and are finding it difficult to keep them in a crib, I would strongly suggest researching techniques to safely keep your child from climbing out of their crib before attempting to train in a bed (making sure your doctor is okay with any techniques you may want to try). Some parents find success in switching from a crib to a Pack 'n Play, since the mesh sides make it harder for babies to climb up and out. Others check with their pediatricians first that it's okay to put their toddlers in sleep sacks to encumber their legs so that they are unable to climb out of their cribs. If your child is *still* climbing out of their crib, read on.

First, you will need to prepare your child's sleep environment. It should be 100 percent childproofed, with *all* furniture—dressers, bookcases, changing tables—bolted or strapped to the wall (earthquake straps are great). I've heard of children climbing furniture that topples down on them, injuring them or worse. Any other hazards should be removed, including anything a child could choke on or wrap around their necks. Get down on your hands and knees and make sure there is absolutely nothing your child could get their hands on that could cause them harm. Be prepared, too, for the possibility that your child will try to turn on the lights by removing the bulbs from overhead lights and even taking lamps with you once you say good night. Finally, dress your child in such a way that they cannot remove their clothes and/ or diaper. Try cutting the feet off a footed sleeper and put it on backwards so your child isn't able to take it off. As with infants, make sure you are using loud white noise, ensuring as much darkness in the bedroom as possible, and observing your child at all times with a video monitor. Finally, many toddlers prefer to sleep on the floor instead of in their bed in the first few weeks of training, so leave some bedding (a sleeping bag and pillow is usually sufficient) by the door in case that's where your child decides they want to sleep.

At some point, you will need to be prepared to keep your child in their room through more drastic means, including a gate at the door, a toddler safety doorknob cover, or a doorknob with a lock facing the hallway instead of into the room. Many parents balk at the idea of "locking" a child in their room, yet think nothing of confining them to a crib. It makes more sense to think of it in terms of keeping a child in a fully safe place (their bedroom), just like you kept them in their crib. The real safety issue around this age is when a child is not only unable to fall asleep unassisted, but they also are able to leave their bedroom at will. Toddlers are exposed to all sorts of risks when they have the freedom to come and go as they please, and are safer confined to a bedroom than having free range of the house in the middle of the night.

Of all the methods available to keep your child safely in their bedroom, I highly suggest you choose the doorknob cover. A gate may seem more humane, but it usually just compels a child to stand at the door for long periods of time as they cry into the house to get your attention. A lock is effective, but unnecessary; a doorknob cover works just as well. With older children especially, a cover seems to upset them less than a locked door. If your doors have levers as handles, I recommend switching to a doorknob for your child's room, as the commercially-available handle covers for knobs are much more effective than the ones available for levers. Consider investing in a toddler clock that lights up a certain color when it's time to start each morning.

Finally, select one of the following ways to show your child the number of chances they have to choose to stay in their bed until the morning. The first will work best for children who like to sleep with their door open, and the second is better for kids who prefer to sleep with their door closed.

For kids who like to sleep with the door open, you will want to open your child's bedroom door until it is at a forty-five-degree angle to the threshold and place a piece of masking tape directly underneath where the door is over the floor. Close it about one-quarter of the way towards the threshold and place another piece of tape, another one-quarter with a piece of tape, another one-quarter with a piece of tape, and place one final piece of tape on the threshold itself (where the door is when closed). There should be five pieces of tape total, marking the door open at a ninety-degree angle, then at the 1/4, 1/2, 3/4, and fully closed marks.

Children who prefer to sleep with their door closed should have four sticky notes placed high up on their side of the door.

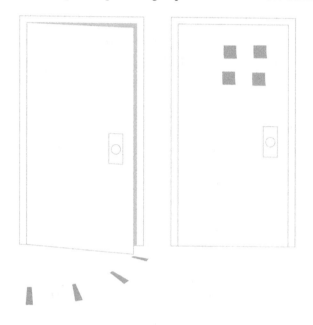

The final preparation is to create a large, colorful sticker chart on a poster board, with columns representing days, and rows representing every conceivable activity you do with your child prior to going to sleep, starting with dinner (i.e., bath, pajamas, books, kisses, etc.). Add all the activities your child usually asks for as excuses to try to leave their bedroom, like a drink of water or using the potty. This is not a traditional sticker chart in that there is no benefit to finishing the chart. Instead, it serves as a visual checklist for your family.

Don't discuss these preparations with your child. Later on, you will explain what everything means, but play off the importance of these changes if your child sees them before starting sleep training.

At dinner on the first night of training, present your child with the chart, excitedly exclaiming that from now on you will be using it before bed to make sure you do all the things you need to do before going to sleep. Don't mention anything about sleep training or "staying in bed"—simply act like this is a fun, new thing you will be doing, and make sure you use stickers that will be particularly enticing to your child.

After dinner, it's time to begin. Start at the top of the chart and work your way down. As you go through each activity, do not linger on any one. When you ask, for example, if your child wants a sip of water, ask, "Would you like a drink of water?" If they ignore you or won't answer, ask them one more time, this time adding, "Do you want a drink of water? If you don't take your chance now, that's it; you won't get another chance until the morning." Regardless of their response or non-response, add a sticker to the chart and do not go back. Also, don't be too serious about the stickers—if your child wants one on his shirt for every one placed on the chart, that's just fine. If your child shouts for a drink of water later, let them know they had their chance; instead, leave them a sippy cup of water in their bedroom so they can have access to it overnight.

Once you have finished all of your bedtime activities, clearly explain to your child that from now on you will be sleeping in your bed until the morning and that they need to stay in their room, in their bed, until the morning as well. Make sure that this is clear to your child while not dwelling on it any longer than necessary. Show them the toddler clock and explain that when it lights up that will mean it's time to start the day. At this point, explain either the tape marks on the floor or the sticky notes on the door. Tell your child that if they get out of bed once, the door will be closed to the first mark (or, the first sticky note will be removed), and for each time they leave their room, the door will be closed or you will remove a note, until the door is closed all the way, or the sticky notes are all gone. Then explain that once the door is closed, "it will remain closed until the morning," when the toddler clock goes off. Don't show your child the toddler doorknob cover or explain how it works or that they won't be able to open it. If you are using the sticky method, make sure that after removing each sticky note, you leave the door *almost* closed, but not closed all the way, since you want to allow your child to exercise their ability to actually open the door such that once the door is closed, they understand that they need to stay in their bedroom until morning. Regardless of your child's reaction, work hard to remain calm and neutral. Give your child a kiss, tell them you love them, leave, and follow the directions each time they leave the room. As they leave their room and lose their "chances," walk them back to bed calmly, telling them you love them and that you'll see them in the morning. It is vital that through this training process you remain happy and neutral, and never give in to arguing, cajoling, begging, or arguing. Simply move down the list and proceed towards bedtime.

A surprising number of children only need one or two door closings or sticky note removals before deciding to stay in their rooms... often while throwing a fit. As long as your child stays in their room, do not continue to remove their chances by closing the door in increments or taking away sticky notes. I have known children to fall asleep with their head over the threshold of the doorway, and their parents and I have counted that as a success! As long as your child stays in their room and falls asleep unassisted, it does not matter where they go to sleep.

If your child exhausts all of their chances at bedtime, you must follow through by shutting the door and leaving it closed until the morning. *Do not interact or speak with your child through the door, and do not give them any more chances.* Watch them closely through the monitor, and as long as they remain safe, leave them be. Keep the door closed until the toddler clock goes off. Some toddlers have been known to cry or protest for hours, but the vast majority of the time, if you implement this method exactly as outlined, children will take only thirty to sixty minutes to fall asleep.

If your child uses a few chances, then falls asleep, only

to wake up and leave their room in the middle of the night, start wherever you left off, walk them back to their room and take away another one of the chances. No drama or engaging, just put them back to bed and move on.

As with all aspects of sleep training, at every age, being consistent is your most important job. The fantastic thing about sleep training toddlers is that they usually get it, and fast! Nighttime training often takes just one or two nights and then you are done, assuming you simultaneously implement nap training and remain consistent in insisting that your child fall asleep totally unassisted.

> A note on going potty: There are very few things that young children are truly in control of, and going poop or potty is one of them. Admittedly, sleep training is much easier to implement when your child is still in diapers or training-style disposable underwear. In fact, my own children and those of most of my clients stay in diapers or training underwear through age four, all the while being wholly and easily potty-trained during the daytime. It is a myth that in order for your child to be successfully potty trained during the day, they must be potty trained at night. However, if you find yourself sleep training your child while they are in underwear, you will need to balance their need to go to the bathroom

with expecting them to stay in their room. If your child can be trusted, you can try to put a small potty in their bedroom; that way, if they need to use it, they can do so on their own. Or, you can implement a rule of allowing them to go once before midnight and once afterwards. If they ask for potty, you take them, and they don't go, they will likely have an accident later. Have them help you clean it up and move on. If your child continues to use going potty as an excuse to stay awake, strongly consider putting them back in a diaper or training underwear overnight. I have never once had a child regress with potty training as a result of returning to diapers overnight.

Nap Training

When it comes to nap training toddlers, the name of the game is stamina (and, as always, consistency). About eighty percent of toddlers will adapt to nap training in the first three days, with the remaining twenty percent going on a complete nap strike for up to sixteen days. Stay strong! Toddlers will resume napping if you are consistent; stay the course and give the process time.

Since children at this stage will be taking just one nap each day, you will be implementing up to three one-hour nap attempts each day, making certain your child does not fall asleep in the car or anywhere other than the bed while they work on learning to fall asleep consistently at home. As with crib training, do not begin sleep training until your child can remain 100 percent at home (with no outings whatsoever for any reason) for the first forty-eight to seventy-two hours of the sleep training process.

Depending on what time your child typically naps, I would suggest making your first attempt around 11:00 a.m. or noon. Using the same chart and door/tape or sticky note method, put your child down for a nap and give them up to one hour to fall asleep. If they are unsuccessful, get them up for a thirty-minute break, then put them down again for another hour. If they are still unsuccessful, make one final attempt, then keep them up until bedtime. If they do fall asleep at any point, get them up as soon as they wake on their own. Even if the nap is short, don't attempt any more naps that day.

You may find that your child does better when they are given two ninety-minute attempts instead of three one-hour attempts. This is also an effective form of nap training, as it gives children a little more time to try to fall asleep on their own.

It is very, very important that you never allow you child to fall asleep anywhere other than their room during sleep training. Do not give in and help them take a nap because they need a "break" and haven't been able to fall asleep. One of the secrets of the Baby Sleep Trainer Method is allowing the body to re-regulate its own daytime sleep. The only way to interfere with that process is by allowing or encouraging your child to sleep in the car or stroller, or anywhere other than their own bed.

If your child is in daycare during the day, you're in luck! Almost without fail, toddlers in daycare nap very well, even if they nap poorly at home on the weekends. Generally, it's the "mass mentality" of all their peers sleeping that encourages them go to sleep on their own. I would encourage you to implement nap training on the weekends to encourage your child to nap well when they're with you as well.

If your child is no longer napping, proceed with nighttime training and skip the nap training altogether.

What to do if your child is not yet old enough to "understand" the bed training method

I considered ignoring this issue altogether, because training children out of a crib between the ages of seventeen months and two-and-a-half years appears relatively unsophisticated and unnecessarily harsh. However, I want to be able to provide help for those who find themselves in this difficult situation. Know first that it *is* possible to train children in this age group, as long as you are consistent in implementing the following guidelines.

1. Childproofing is extremely important. Follow the recommendations outlined above (securing furniture, using a video monitor, etc.).

2. Skip the chart and tape/Post-It Notes and instead follow the recommendations outlined for bedtime routines in the crib training chapter.

3. After the five-minute soothing technique, put them down in their bed, walk out of the room, and close the door. Be sure that it is secured shut with a toddler doorknob cover.

4. Unless your child is in danger, do not respond to them through the door. In order for training to be successful in this age group, you will need to do full "extinction" style training with no checks. It is *imperative* that you be able to see your child through a video monitor throughout the entire process. If you find yourself needing to enter the room for any reason, simply address whatever need your child has, then leave again, and close the door. Their door should remain closed until the time you deem is the start of their day.

Because this is the most hands-off method in this book, it should absolutely not be implemented without the consent of your pediatrician. Many families simply choose to delay training until their toddler is closer to two-and-a-half years in order to avoid this type of training. Know, however, that if your pediatrician approves this method, you should consider it safe and effective. For nap training, follow the guidelines above, but simply close the door instead of using the tape or Post-It Note technique.

Remember that sleep training a toddler will almost always come down to a standoff of some sort. Be strong for your child, and maintain the necessary structure in your home to help them be the successful independent sleepers they need to be. If you have endured months or years of poor sleep, know that sleep training will ultimately require less effort that whatever you are already doing and will culminate with you giving your child the precious gift of getting all the sleep their bodies truly need to grow, learn, and thrive!

CONGRATS!

YOU'VE DONE IT!

You have spent your time educating and preparing yourself to successfully sleep train your child with the fewest tears possible. I want to genuinely extend my thanks for trusting me and following my advice, and to remind you again that all you need to be successful is time, patience, consistency, and faith. Please feel free to follow Baby Sleep Trainer at;

www.facebook.com/babysleeptrainer

or reach out to me directly for one-on-one support at;

www.babysleeptrainer.com.

Made in the USA
Monee, IL
15 August 2020

38430112R00075